Praise for
Let's Talk Race

Let's Talk Race is a solid and very practical guide to having the necessary conversations that those of us who are white are so reluctant to have with our families, friends, neighbors, and co-workers. This book will motivate you to break white silence and will support you in addressing the racism that engulfs our communities and diminishes all of our lives.

—Paul Kivel, educator, activist, author, *Uprooting Racism:
How White People Can Work for Racial Justice, 4th edition*

Let's Talk Race is wisely conceived and masterfully accomplished. Both a primer on cultural competence and a charge to engage in genuine conversation, this book is candidly honest, brilliantly transparent, and a phenomenal resource. The two authors are grounded in decades of experience, girded with wisdom and courage, and guided by a commitment to illuminate hope in the presence of fear. This is a *must* read!

—Emmett G. Price III, Ph.D., Executive Director, Institute for the Study of the Black Christian Experience, Gordon Conwell Theological Seminary

Let's Talk Race can be part of our national racial reckoning. White mothers—like Johnson and Fine—raising Black male children straddle double consciousness where racial blindness and liberal platitudes are dangerous. The book intentionally speaks to a white audience. The hard work of talk and struggle are necessary for a white reconciling of historical facts to the current harmful narrative. *Let's Talk Race* is a step along a long journey to truth and reconciliation.

—Tom Shapiro, Pokross Professor of Law and Social Policy, The Heller School for Social Policy, Brandeis University, and author, *Toxic Inequality, The Hidden Cost of Being African American,* and *Black Wealth/White Wealth*

Drawing on both the best of interracial communication research and their personal experiences as white women who have navigated countless interracial conversations, Johnson and Fine illuminate the barriers to such conversations and provide practical and accessible strategies for overcoming those barriers. No book is more relevant to everyday life in the socially diverse world of 21st-century America than *Let's Talk Race*.

—Marsha Houston, Professor, Communication Studies, retired, University of Alabama, Tuscaloosa, and co-editor, *Our Voices: Essays in Culture, Ethnicity, and Communication* and *Centering Ourselves: African American Feminist and Womanist Studies of Discourse*

Let's Talk Race is a seminal book for this time. It is a desperately needed resource that will help our nation heal and live into its noblest ideals. Four hundred years after the start of slavery, America is having a racial awakening and beginning to reckon with the consequences of founding the nation on genocide, stolen land, and slave labor. As the country shakes off the husks of complacency and indifference, people of all races, creeds, colors, religions, and national origin are discovering an unprecedented opportunity to realize the aspiration of justice in the first sentence of the Constitution of the United States. If justice is to be realized, white America must stand in transformative solidarity with those who face the burdens of structural racism. This book provides a practical yet soul-enriching path forward to move from talk to action with grace, empathy, and a commitment to usher in an era of just and fair inclusion into a society in which we can all participate, prosper, and reach our full potential.

—Dr. Michael McAfee, President and CEO, PolicyLink

Ever the teachers, Marlene and Fern take care to scaffold the learning so that readers are able to build a strong foundation upon which to grow. While some of the information seems basic to me as a Black woman, I appreciate the importance of more white folks talking to one another about race because they understand the blind spots, the pit falls, the traps, and what I call "trash thinking," that needs to be composted. I hope readers enjoy the personal storytelling, the Do's and Don'ts lists, and the personal reflection prompts that are included throughout the book. Finally, I hope more of us reach a point when talking about race can be "cathartic, healing, and joyful."

—Desiraé Simmons, Co-director, Interfaith Council for
Peace and Justice, Ann Arbor, MI

We are 21 years into the 21st century and yet W. E. B. Du Bois' pre-science haunts us: the problem of the color line is still here, painful, and seemingly indelible. That line is ever-present, separating those who will live from those who will die by acts of police violence; dividing those to be grieved from those deemed disposable; privileging those who are white while marginalizing and damning those who are Black. *Let's Talk Race* is a socially, politically, and existentially urgent book that details the painful reality of America's race evasion. With a call for fearless speech and courageous listening, the authors of this demanding and yet inviting book refuse to be complicit with white silence, apathy, and ignorance. The title's invitation requires vulnerability, signifies a space for collective mourning, and is honest about the profound risks in-volved. The authors, Fern L. Johnson and Marlene G. Fine, recognize the daring and radical loving requisite for talking about race and facing America's original sin.

—George Yancy, Professor, Samuel Candler Dobbs, Emory University

People of color and African Americans are beyond aware and are experiencing racial fatigue after a lifetime and decades of attempting to educate peers, colleagues, friends, and strangers about the reality of racism and its impact on every aspect of their/our daily lives. We are at a pivotal time in which white people need to become actively engaged in authentic conversations about race. *Let's Talk Race* is a great resource for these difficult conversations because it contains practical advice while also providing readers with a wealth of vital information grounded in facts and from reliable sources. Our country and world are in dire need of resources such as this, and I am excited to add it to my library and scholarship.

—Dr. Tina M. Harris, Professor, Manship-Maynard Endowed Chair of Race, Media, and Cultural Literacy, Louisiana State University, Manship School of Mass Communication

LET'S TALK
RACE

a guide for white people

FERN L. JOHNSON ▪ MARLENE G. FINE

new society
PUBLISHERS

Cover design by Diane McIntosh.
Cover art ©iStock; Sidebar background © AdobeStock_91380585
Printed in Canada. First printing April 2021.

Inquiries regarding requests to reprint all or part of *Let's Talk Race* should be addressed to New Society Publishers at the address below. To order directly from the publishers, please call toll-free (North America) 1-800-567-6772, or order online at www.newsociety.com

Any other inquiries can be directed by mail to:

New Society Publishers
P.O. Box 189, Gabriola Island, BC V0R 1X0, Canada
(250) 247-9737

LIBRARY AND ARCHIVES CANADA CATALOGUING IN PUBLICATION
Title: Let's talk race : a guide for white people / Fern L. Johnson and Marlene G. Fine.
Names: Johnson, Fern L., author. | Fine, Marlene Gail, 1949- author.
Description: Includes bibliographical references and index.
Identifiers: Canadiana (print) 20200360620 | Canadiana (ebook) 20200360663 | ISBN 9780865719538
   (softcover) | ISBN 9781550927467 (PDF) | ISBN 9781771423427 (EPUB)
Subjects: LCSH: Racism. | LCSH: Whites—Race identity. | LCSH: Race. | LCSH: Race awareness. | LCSH: Privilege (Social psychology)
Classification: LCC HT1521 .J64 2021 | DDC 305.8—dc23

Funded by the Government of Canada | Financé par le gouvernement du Canada | Canada

New Society Publishers' mission is to publish books that contribute in fundamental ways to building an ecologically sustainable and just society, and to do so with the least possible impact on the environment, in a manner that models this vision.

MIX
Paper from responsible sources
FSC
www.fsc.org FSC® C016245

Certified
B Corporation

new society
PUBLISHERS

Contents

For Julius and Will

Acknowledgments

WE BELIEVE IN THE POWER OF CONVERSATION to shape ideas, build relationships, and mobilize action. The hundreds of conversations about race that we've had over the years brought us to the ideas presented in this book. We are especially grateful to our many students for their willingness to talk about race, often by taking personal risks. Marlene is particularly grateful to her colleagues and participants in the YW Boston Dialogues on Race and Ethnicity who taught her so much about the importance of listening to people's stories. We feel enormously privileged to have had so many friends and colleagues who shared ideas, personal experiences, and opinions with us. To the many academic and literary writers whose work engages race, we offer thanks for putting your ideas out there for public consumption and conversation.

Writing this book felt risky because we knew that we needed to strike a delicate balance to engage white readers without alienating them and to talk about the history and experiences of Blacks and other people of color without speaking for them. We hoped to open up the conversation about race, especially for white people, but we didn't want to position ourselves as having "the answer." We asked a number of people whom we could count on for blunt feedback and constructive suggestions to read draft chapters. We thank them for their comments and questions, and for raising issues we missed: Bill DeMuth, Christy Egun-Badger, Bill Erklauer, Marsha Houston, Linda Meyer, Janet Rickles,

Janet Stiller, and Angie Woodmansee. Your engagement with our project was a valuable gift.

Many family members, friends, and colleagues willingly responded when we needed help or to test an idea. Many thanks to Carolyn Anderson, Judith Aronson, Rhea Becker, Richard Beenen, Angela Bazydlo, Ellen Benevides, Lois Brynes, Debbie Dawson, Gail Dines, Cynthia Enloe, Karen Foss, Joani Geltman, Laurie Hayes, Serena Hilsinger, Ben Ho, Jennifer Ho, Martin Ho, Mary Ho, Jake Kiakahi, Richard Leland, David Levy, Stephen Littlejohn, Marilyn Lucchi, Mary Nyquist, Deb Osborne, Alan Osborne, Ousmane Power-Green, Christopher Ricks, Barb Sweeney, Kimi Takesue, and so many others.

Our dear friend Margo Melnicove read every word of our draft chapters, casting her expert journalistic eye on our writing, helping us bring our academic style into more readable prose, asking questions that forced us to sharpen our arguments, and offering constant encouragement.

Everyone at New Society Publishers was helpful and responsive. Special thanks to Rob West, Acquisitions Editor, for your confidence from the beginning in our project, for sharing ideas that strengthened the book, and most of all for your humane sensibility and empathy at every step of the process right through the stress of the pandemic and the horror of racial events in the US. To all those involved in production and marketing, thanks for your part: Diane McIntosh, Alina Cerminara, Sue Custance, EJ Hurst, Mary Jane Jessen, Sara Reeves, and our copy editor, Judith Brand.

Most importantly, we thank our sons, William and Julius, who teach us every day about living as Black men in the US and who have enriched our lives and helped us see the world differently.

Introduction

WE BEGAN JOTTING DOWN NOTES for this book early in 2016. By that time reports of the police shooting of Michael Brown in Ferguson, Missouri, had been followed by far too many news flashes of yet another senseless shooting of a Black person. Our notes took more shape before Donald Trump was elected president in November 2016. The months leading up to the election and the first few months of his presidency convinced us even more that it was urgent that whites learn how to talk about race with each other and with people of color. White supremacists boldly asserted themselves in the early days of the Trump presidency. The movement increasingly felt comfortable going public. Then came the August 2017 "Unite the Right" rally of white supremacists and neo-Nazis in Charlottesville, Virginia, with the president of the United States pronouncing that there were "very fine people on both sides." We started writing at a faster pace as racist graffiti sprung up around the country, more Black shootings by police occurred, and anti-immigration rhetoric became official government policy. As we came closer to completing our manuscript, the coronavirus pandemic struck the world. As we write this introduction, we are at the height of the deadliest weeks and months for virus cases and deaths in the US. We are under a directive from our governor to remain in our home, able to leave only for groceries or medicine, advised to wear face masks in public, and maintaining contact with family and friends only through telephone and computer. And more news of the disproportional death count among Black and brown people is piling up.

The irony of writing about face-to-face conversation in the age of the coronavirus is not lost on us. The social changes to come as a result of the pandemic are unknown. We may be talking with others only online and by phone for some time to come, and it's possible that we will not be sitting close together in a circle or around a table for the foreseeable future. We hope the crisis will end eventually, and we will be able to talk again face-to-face.

Several terms that we use throughout the book need to be defined and clarified. First, we frequently refer to both "race" and "ethnicity"— terms that can be confusing. Because we often report demographic information gathered by the US Census Bureau, we use most of their terms. Census Bureau questionnaires ask respondents to identify their race and to indicate if they are of Hispanic, Latino, or Spanish origin. *Race* is defined as a person's self-identification with one or more social groups. The race categories used by the Census Bureau are: White; Black or African American; American Indian or Alaska Native; Chinese; Filipino; Asian Indian; Vietnamese; Korean; Japanese; other Asian; Native Hawaiian, Samoan; Chamorro; other Pacific Islander; and some other race. A person can select more than one category. Reports frequently present data for only three groupings: White, Black (which includes African Americans and others who identify as Black), and Asian (which includes different groups lumped together). The smaller groupings are reported separately.

"Ethnicity" as used by the Census Bureau is easily misunderstood. The "ethnicity question" asks people to indicate whether or not they are Hispanic, which is defined as being of Hispanic, Latino, or Spanish origin. On the census form, the category includes: Mexican; Mexican American; Chicano; Puerto Rican; Cuban; and another Hispanic, Latino, or Spanish origin (for example, Colombian or Dominican). "Hispanic," therefore, is an ethnic category reflecting a person's heritage or nationality, and not a race. A person can identify as a Black Hispanic or a white Hispanic, which is why there are references to non-Hispanic whites or non-Hispanic Blacks in many reports. In general usage, the category is often mislabeled as a racial designation.

Second, we have made three decisions regarding naming. One is to use Latinx rather than Hispanic or Latino. "Hispanic" technically refers to people from Spanish-speaking countries, which is not the case for many people counted by the Census Bureau as Hispanic, such as Brazilians who speak Portuguese or Haitians who speak French. The term "Latino" technically refers to males but is used as a generic for males and females. "Latina" can be used for females, but "Latinx" recognizes men, women, trans, and non-binary people of Latin descent. Throughout the book, you will see both Hispanic and Latino in the text. In those instances, we are maintaining the terms used by the original source of the material.

Our second decision about naming is to capitalize "Black" while keeping "white" in lower case. After reading what journalists and academics had to say about the issue, we decided to capitalize Black. For example, Brian McGrory, the editor of the *Boston Globe*, sent an email to his staff in January 2020 telling them that the paper would depart from Associated Press Style and begin using the capital B "to recognize that the word has evolved from a description of a person's skin color to signify a race and a culture, and as such, deserves uppercase treatment." W.E.B. DuBois made the same argument a century before. In the mid-1920s, DuBois began a letter-writing campaign demanding that publishers, newspapers, and magazines capitalize Negro as a way to confer respect. Mainstream publications eventually agreed. In 1930, the *New York Times* announced that they would capitalize Negro "in recognition of racial respect for those who have been generations in the 'lower case.'" Over the next decades, Negro was replaced by African American and then Black. Over time, many publications moved to lowercase black, most likely because white was written in lower case—the exception being in white nationalist materials. As publications struggled with the issue, most dictionaries and style manuals advised using lower case because black and white signified broad descriptions of skin color rather than ethnicity or origin. Nearly ninety years after the *New York Times'* decision to capitalize Negro, journalist Lori Tharps wrote an editorial calling for the capitalization of Black, saying "We are indeed a people, a race, a tribe. It's only correct."[1] We agree. We also agree that it is important to capitalize Black but keep white in lower case because "leaving white in lowercase represents a righting of a long-standing wrong and a demand for dignity and racial equity."[2] Capitalizing Black while not capitalizing white is a linguistic means of redressing both the historical and present-day marginalization of people of color.

Our third decision about naming is to use both "slave" and "enslaved" throughout the book as well as "enslaver" rather than "owner." Some historians now prefer "enslaved" because it identifies people as humans with agency before identifying them as commodities. We move between these terms. Sometimes we want to recognize that the enslaved resisted their servitude, acted in secret, and took risks. Other times, we want to emphasize the dehumanization of slavery. We use "enslavers" rather than "owners" in order to hold those individuals accountable for their inhumanity.

Finally, although we refer often to "people of color," we are primarily writing about Black people's lives and experiences and how to talk with ourselves and with Black people about race. In some places, we give examples related to other racial categories and Latinx people, but the bulk of our writing concerns Blacks. We also believe that, while all racial disparities must be redressed, the disparities between Blacks and whites are particularly damaging to the fabric of the nation because they were sewn in from our inception and have continued to fray for centuries. We will come apart at the seams if we do not repair the damage. Much of what we say, however, can be extrapolated to other racial groups, although the specifics vary. The same type of maligning and stereotyping of Black people to position them as "other" can be seen elsewhere. Native Americans, Muslims, and peoples of differing Latinx and Asian backgrounds are called vile names, profiled, and threatened. Case in point: the president of the United States called COVID-19 "the Chinese virus," casting a pall over Chinese Americans and other Chinese people living in the US. Before social distancing became a reality, Chinese restaurants were shunned. Reports abound today of Chinese people and others who look Asian being subjected to name-calling, taunting, threats, and violence.

Finally, a few comments about our voices as writers of this book. Most important, we are the white mothers of African American adult sons, whom we adopted as infants. We have learned about race over the journey of parenthood. Both of us also have academic expertise in issues related to race and culture. We wrote this book mainly for white people. We have tried not to make statements that generalize about Black people or any other race or ethnic group unless those statements are rooted in research that can be verified, in our personal experiences as members of an interracial family, in personal testimonies and beliefs that we quote or summarize, or in what we have been told by Black people.

Writing this book was a labor of love for us—a reaching out for commitments to create better racial understanding. Raising two Black sons taught us much about racism and about the need for white people to be able to talk about race openly and non-defensively. We approached our work with a sense of excitement and urgency. Our research and writing became more and more difficult as we dug deeply into the reality of racism—its violence, its virulence, and the ways it is embedded throughout our institutions and our social and political lives—and the stark realization that it continues just as virulently today. As much as we've learned over the years, we were often overwhelmed by sadness at the end of a day of writing, sadness that was compounded by knowing that what we as white people were reading and writing about is the lived experience of many Black people in the US. We hope that you will approach this book with an open mind and an open heart. A mind open to learning about the lives and experiences of people of color and a heart filled with compassion for those lives and experiences.

We are hopeful that people will resume in-person conversations once the coronavirus crisis is under control, but we're concerned that once again race will be pushed aside. It's easier to talk about other things because race is fraught with emotional triggers. But the coronavirus pandemic has exposed the fault lines in the experiences of whites and people of color. Early data show that Blacks are dying at over twice the rate of whites. The data are not surprising. Black people tend to live in crowded, low-income neighborhoods. They often work in low-level service jobs with high face-to-face requirements: caregivers, bus drivers, health care workers, supermarket staff, gas station attendants, restaurant workers. Fewer have health insurance and adequate access to health care. The experience of the Great Recession suggests that Blacks and Latinx will fall further behind economically when we emerge into what may be a prolonged recession. We hope that our readers will not push race aside but, instead, will seek out conversations about race and partners with whom to have those conversations. If social distancing continues, even to a lesser degree, we will need to be creative about using communications technologies to connect with others, both friends and strangers. Achieving racial equity and harmony demands that we find ways to start and sustain talking to each other. We hope the material in the following pages will be a guide to doing that.

Chapter 1

Bridging the Chasm

Starting the Conversation about Race

"Until we start talking about what we believe and
why we believe it, we will continue to tiptoe around
each other and get nowhere. We have seen what the
silence does. We should give talking a chance."

—Claudia Rankine, discussing her play *The White Card*

RANKINE IS TALKING ABOUT THE SILENCE about race—a silence
sustained by skillful evasion and indirection. She made these comments in an interview about her play *The White Card*. The play features
four upper-class whites (a married couple and their college-age son,
and a male friend of the couple) and a Black woman photographer
whose work the couple is interested in purchasing. The play opens
on a note of civility and devolves into racial animosity. After stilted
back-and-forth interaction washed down with champagne, the veneer
of civility cracks, exposing deep racial division. Rankine's play is an invitation to talk and break the silence about race. That invitation is ever
more urgent today as support for the Black Lives Matter movement
grows.

Rankine titles her play to call out a hidden, yet powerful, story
about race in America. We are familiar with the expression "playing the
race card." The phrase is most often used to disparage people of color
or their advocates and to discredit claims of racism. When Rankine
turns the expression toward whites, she exposes how some whites

promote their "good" views on race without admitting their own white biases:

- "I support police reform."
- "I work every day to do the right thing."
- "I'm not a racist. I'm color blind."

Rankine's play puts a lens up to some of the ways white people don't understand the implications of their comments, behaviors, and attitudes about race. As she says, it's now time for "giving talking a chance."[1]

This book takes up Rankine's urgent message to give talk a chance, because if we don't, we will never achieve social and economic justice. We address white people because, collectively, we have not dug deeply enough to get past our ignorance, embarrassment, and fears about race. We are writing from our perspective as two white women who are the mothers of two African American men who were adopted as infants.[2] Throughout the years of parenting, we came to understand at least some of what it means to be Black in this country and some of what it means to be the parents of Black children. We learned from books, workshops, talking with Black friends and acquaintances, and the minutiae of everyday life. We learned from how our children were treated on playgrounds and at school, from what was said about our being "such good people" for adopting Black children, from suspicious glances at our family, from unexpected stereotypes directed at our children. A white woman at a concert we attended with the boys when they were in middle school asked if they were the Lost Boys of Sudan. We learned from Black friends that our children would be subjected to having their hair touched by white children and even adults without permission. That teachers would set low expectations for their academic performance and high ones for their athletic performance. That we would have to teach our boys how to behave when they were pulled over by the police when driving. And we learned that they *would* be pulled over by the police. We also learned over and over how much we did not and still do not understand, and how easy it was and continues to be surprised by our ignorance.

We believe that talking about race is imperative but requires commitment to listen, willingness to entertain new ideas, and openness to learning that one's thinking about many aspects of race has been wrong—often harmfully wrong. If we do not talk about race, then our ideas remain private and passively influenced by media images and what we might read about race. If we do not talk about race for fear of saying the wrong thing, then the unsaid is allowed to speak for itself. Yet, before we can engage productively with one another, we need to examine why whites find it so hard to talk about race.

Racial barriers stand firm. We need to learn why those barriers exist and how we can diminish them to achieve racial justice and equity. We need to ask—and answer—why do we continue to exist in racial boxes, which set up boundaries and barriers that persist today? If I as a white person fear that I will say the wrong thing, how does that create a barrier? If I as a white person know little about the distribution of wealth among races in our country, how does that create a barrier? If I as a white person say that I do not see color, how does that create a barrier? Barriers in these examples are created by fear in the first case, ignorance in the second, and lack of empathy in the third.

The worst culprit is likely the physical barrier of separation in neighborhoods. We cannot know and understand other people if we do not have contact with them. The housing barrier creates divisions in education, occupation, lifestyle, and health. The United States continues to be residentially segregated, even though there has been slight progress in recent years. Federal, state, and local policies created a suburban-urban split, with people of color concentrated in urban areas. Large metropolitan areas in the North and Midwest, such as Milwaukee, New York, Chicago, Detroit, Cleveland, and Buffalo, have the highest levels of segregation. Within those areas, neighborhood boundaries function like signposts to show who lives where. Rural America, which accounts for slightly less than one-fifth of the US population, is close to 80% white.[3] We will discuss this topic more in chapter 4, but for now, we want to stress that the barriers between races will not be brought down until and unless we acknowledge them, learn about them, discuss their existence, and willingly do something to diminish them.

Our book calls on white people to talk with one another and with people of color about race and to explore why whites have such a difficult time in conversations about race. If we can't talk among ourselves, how will we ever be able to talk constructively across racial boundaries? We, as white people, need to talk frankly, respectfully, and without defensiveness. We view talk among white people as essential to gaining the courage and skill to talk across the racial divide. And we view talk across race as essential to building the trust, understanding, and relationships essential to achieving racial equity.

We imagine that some people will respond to this call by thinking that we're already saturated with talk about race. It's true that news, politics, social media, TV shows, and movies prominently focus on race, but that's not the same as talking deeply about race. Researchers who explored race relations in office settings remarked that "Americans talk about race all the time but usually through code and allusion."[4] To talk about race means more than simply saying something about the topic, lumping everything together with blanket terms like "diversity" and "multicultural," or alluding to "problems" that involve those who are somehow marked as different from whites. For us, talking about race means to engage, to probe, and to have respectful and sustained conversations that focus on what, why, and how we think about race and our experiences with it. Talk in this sense is a personal and social responsibility to probe questions such as: Why are we reluctant to get too deeply into race talk, or to even broach topics related to race? What are our personal and family histories with race? What is okay or not okay to say when talking about race to other white people and to people of other races? What don't we know about race, and why don't we know it?

The context for writing and talking about race is continuously reshaped by current events. President Bill Clinton, for instance, called in 1997 for Town Halls around the country to address issues of race and promote racial understanding. Over twenty years later, the national call remains, but in a different and ever more urgent context.

We are writing this book during Donald Trump's presidency. Had we written about the difficulties that whites experience in broaching deep and sustained conversations about race after Barack Obama's election in 2008, the context would have differed. Many held the then-popular belief that race was receding as a significant social problem, and that the election provided evidence of a "post-racial" society. (We never believed this to be the case.) The post-racial idea gave comfort to many whites and provided a kind of relief that the worst of racial injustice was history and a new era was beginning.

At the same time, however, Obama's election unleashed virulent racism that many whites in the US thought no longer existed. Ugly cartoons of the president and first lady circulated on the internet, racist graffiti could be found in most cities and in many schools, and those who claimed the illegitimacy of Obama's birthright as an American never ceased in their assertions. Racism, it seemed, became more rather than less prevalent in our society. Then the startling succession of Black men being shot by police officers galvanized national attention. These shootings, more than anything else, opened a wide chasm in white and Black viewpoints.

It's impossible to pinpoint an exact starting date, but February 26, 2012, stands out. On that day, Trayvon Martin, a seventeen-year-old African American boy, was shot and killed in Florida by George Zimmerman, a mixed-race twenty-eight-year-old. The killing became a subject of controversy when it was reported that Trayvon Martin was unarmed, and George Zimmerman had a history of calling police to report suspicious activity in the gated community where he lived—increasingly identified by Zimmerman as the activity of Black persons. After Zimmerman was acquitted on all charges, protests occurred in many cities, and the racial chasm widened. The *Washington Post* concluded that "the verdict did little to close the stark divisions the case opened up among Americans along the jagged fissures of race and personal safety."[5] The Martin case firmly anchored what was to become all too common news of events in which Blacks were killed by police at the time of an incident or died while in police custody. A narrative of division in how Black people and white people viewed the role of race in the shootings also unfolded.

Signs of racial division intensified following the shooting of Michael Brown on August 9, 2014, in Ferguson, Missouri, and the riots that followed. Shortly after Brown's death, the Pew Research Center released polling data that showed a sharp racial divide in views about what happened and its implications. One finding revealed that 80% of Blacks who were polled thought the shooting raised racial issues, while only 37% of whites held that opinion.[6] The survey also found that more Blacks (76%) than whites (52%) had confidence in the investigations of the shooting. Three points about such survey data deserve comment. First, none of these statistics shows a complete dichotomy between races. Some whites express viewpoints similar to the majority of Blacks, just as some Blacks see things similarly to the majority of whites. Second, answers to any polling question reflect what people think in the particular moment that they answer a question. New events, interactions with others, and personal reflection might lead to a different viewpoint at a different time. Third, none of the statistics are conditioned by probing why a person believes one thing or another or if they hesitated about how to answer.

As news about the shootings exploded, the story of yet another divide emerged, this one of deepening animosity between police advocates and Black community members and their supporters. The deaths of Trayvon Martin and Michael Brown along with the growing unrest about policing launched the Black Lives Matter movement. Signs appeared on buildings and in yards in support of the movement, but opposition also arose with counterclaims that "all lives matter," "white lives matter," and "police lives matter." Whatever a person thought about the events at issue or the Black Lives Matter movement, the names of dead Black people dotted conversations, news stories, and social media:

Tamir Rice—Cleveland, Ohio, 2014
Michael Brown—Ferguson, Missouri, 2014
Eric Garner—Staten Island, New York, 2014

Akai Gurley—Brooklyn, New York, 2014
Walter Scott—N. Charleston, South Carolina, 2015
Freddie Gray—Baltimore, Maryland, 2015
Sandra Bland—Prairie View, Texas, 2015
Philando Castile—Falcon Heights, Minnesota, 2016
Stephon Clark—Sacramento, California, 2018
Antwon Rose II—Pittsburgh, Pennsylvania, 2018
Jimmy Atchison—Atlanta, Georgia, 2019
Elijah McClain—Aurora, Colorado, 2019
Ahmaud Arbery—Brunswick, Georgia, 2020
Breonna Taylor—Louisville, Kentucky, 2020
George Floyd—Minneapolis, Minnesota, 2020
Rayshard Brooks—Atlanta, Georgia, 2020

And the list goes on.

The names became flash points in arguments about racism and justice. Expressions of sympathy and outrage at what was happening were countered by pushback rebutting the contention that Blacks—especially Black men—are more likely than whites to be victimized by police. One such rebuttal in the *National Review,* said: "This narrative [that Black men are overly victimized] is false. In reality, a randomly selected black man is overwhelmingly unlikely to be a victim of police violence—and though white men experience such violence even less often, the disparity is consistent with the racial gap in violent crime, suggesting that the role of racial bias is small."[7] The author continues by offering evidence for his assertions. One might accept or reject the argument or the sources for his evidence, but we can see from his argument where the friction exists.

Replies to the pushback against the Black Lives Matter movement sought to make the point of the movement more exactly. Ronald Sullivan, a Harvard Law School professor, put it this way: "The meme, 'All Lives Matter' is yet another effort to undermine legitimate calls to end antiblack police practices that characterize far too many interactions between police and citizens of color…. All lives, self evidently, matter. That is not the point. The point is that this country has been silent for decades, as citizens of color have been killed by those sworn to protect and serve. The Black Lives Matter movement is an attempt to shed light on a problem that has existed in the shadows."[8]

The pile-up of events and the increasingly polarized commentary that grew around them pointed to a need for better racial understanding and improved race relations. This need was not new, but the accelerated pace of news and social media conveyed an urgency. National leaders spoke out, among them James Comey, then the director of the FBI. Speaking at Georgetown University in 2015, Comey focused his remarks on the strains between Black Americans and law enforcement, saying that the country was "at a crossroads…[where] we can choose to live our everyday lives…hoping someone, somewhere, will do something to ease the tension, to smooth over the conflict. We can roll up our car windows, turn up the radio and drive around these problems, or we can choose to have an open and honest discussion about what our relationship is today—what it should be, what it could be, and what it needs to be—if we took more time to better understand one another."[9]

The ongoing incidents of yet another Black death in a situation involving police sparked more and more calls for a "conversation about race." Cities, organizations, schools and colleges, places of worship, and media outlets ramped up efforts to answer that call. Many of these conversations were probably productive, especially those held in small organizations such as churches and ongoing groups. Yet, what occurred on a larger scale often sounded more like sequential turns at speaking, or perhaps back and forth airing of disagreements among panelists selected by media outlets mainly because they would agree to engage in a point-counterpoint debate-style format—with license to raise their voices. Debate has its purpose and place, but its objective is to win, to dominate, to show superiority of reasoning. This style of discourse seldom brings people together but, rather, moves them apart by accentuating their differences.

An example of a well-intentioned "conversation" event occurred in Boston, where Mayor Marty Walsh launched a series of citywide conversations on race in November 2016. With its fraught history of race, the Boston location was sure to draw interest. Expectations were mixed with promise and cynicism. Held in one of the city's large theatres, a diverse audience packed the space. We recall the local news video footage of people lined up behind the microphone waiting for their turn to speak. The *Boston Globe* characterized the event as "marked by frank and emotional remarks, intense...but also civil."[10] Individuals made their points, and some responded to what had been said previously, but there was little opportunity for true conversation in such a large venue.

Even Starbucks tried to start the race conversation with a campaign launched by its CEO Howard Schulz in 2015 to have baristas write "Race Together" on their customers' coffee cups. The idea was to prompt conversations about race among Starbucks patrons. The campaign met with criticism for being gimmicky, and it ended abruptly.[11] Perhaps the problem was as much the commercialization of the call for conversation as it was the particular gimmick that was used. Yet, the gimmick of writing the invitation may have been a sign that a well-meaning CEO simply did not know how to talk about the topic but felt a responsibility to do something. Fast-forward to an incident on April 12, 2018, that put the company back in the news—this time because two Black men, who had arrived early for a meeting with another person at a Philadelphia Starbucks, were handcuffed and arrested in the store for asking to use the bathroom without ordering anything.[12] The incident brought a vigorous apology from Schulz and a commitment to diversity training for staff in many of its stores. The men settled their case with the City, and Starbucks agreed to pay for their college degree programs and to run diversity training sessions at 8,000 of their locations. (By policy, Starbucks does not require people to make a purchase when in their stores.)

Recent research makes clear that whites and Blacks across the country continue to view race differently. A 2019 Pew report revealed the significance of these differences.[13] The percent of respondents saying that Blacks are treated less fairly than whites is as follows.

- in the workplace: 82% of Blacks and 44% of whites
- when applying for a loan or mortgage: 74% of Blacks and 38% of whites

- by police: 84% of Blacks and 63% of whites
- in the courts: 87% of Blacks and 61% of whites
- in stores or restaurants: 70% of Blacks and 37% of whites
- when voting in elections: 58% of Blacks and 30% of whites

Blacks and whites also differ on the reasons why Blacks have a harder time getting ahead.

- racial discrimination: 84% Blacks and 54% whites
- lower quality schools: 72% Blacks and 60% whites
- lack of high paying jobs: 76% Blacks and 51% whites

Finally, 71% of Blacks compared to 56% of whites believe that race relations are bad. These statistics may not surprise many white people, but others probably wonder why the differences of opinion can be so great. A white person, with no conscious racist intentions, might think that a Black person has an outdated point of view or that they are over-generalizing from personal experience. Or the white person might have no idea whatsoever why Black people feel as they do.

A survey conducted for CNN in early June 2020 provides information on differences between Blacks and whites in the wake of George Floyd's killing and the protest movement that followed.[14] Most of those in the random survey, regardless of their race and ethnicity, believed that peaceful protests were valid, but stark racial differences were recorded about what it means to live as a Black or a white person in the US. Black and white respondents differed substantially on their personal experience. Blacks were less likely than whites:

- to believe that the criminal justice system treats Blacks and whites equally: 6% compared to 29%
- to say that there were times when they felt their life was in danger: 54% compared to 14%
- to believe they were denied a job they were qualified for: 38% compared to 6%

We believe that the dramatic differences in how Blacks and whites view race and report on their personal experiences prove the need for whites to talk more deeply among themselves about race so that we can talk more productively across race. We absolutely need to talk with and learn from people of races different from ours, but there is much work to be done among ourselves to make interracial conversation possible. In our own experiences teaching, conducting workshops, and giving talks, we have heard many Blacks and other people of color express frustration with whites because they repeatedly ask the same questions rather than find answers for themselves, tend to move conversations about race to broader topics that shift the focus away from race, and minimize the significance of personal testimonies by presenting counter examples. We have also found that whites in these contexts often clam up or deflect comments made by people of color. Whites need to talk frankly about how they react when the topic of race comes up when people of color are present, and we need to learn how to keep the conversation on race when that is the focus, rather than shift to wider issues such as class or gender that so easily move the conversation away from race.

The Importance of Genuine Conversation

Before elaborating on the reasons why it is difficult for white people to talk about race, we need to consider why race is important and why we need to talk about it. People take in information and perspectives about race by reading, listening, watching television and movies, and engaging with a range of social media. We also make passing comments about race that we might not think much about, and we have our own private thoughts about race. Most of us do have at least brief conversations about race with others, but these are usually in the context of a problem that has arisen or a dramatic event. Yet, actually talking—by which we mean face-to-face, back-and-forth conversation—is the only way for us to fully understand what we and others mean when we are talking about race. We need genuine conversation in which people clarify their ideas, review and agree on facts, share opinions that they may or may not agree on, and express their feelings. So much of what we say about race is coded and remains hidden without fuller explanation and exploration. We also need to hear each other's stories. Talking about race is often fraught with fear of saying the wrong thing and fear of hearing something hurtful. Conversation allows us to develop trust in others and helps alleviate our fear.

Without getting into an overly technical discussion of conversation, it is useful to distinguish this form of communication from others. Dictionary. com defines *conversation* as "informal interchange of thoughts, information, etc., by spoken words; oral communication between persons." Several key words and aspects of this definition highlight the unique nature of conversation.

First, *conversation is informal*, meaning that it's less bound by prescriptive rules about how to form sentences and use words than are some other forms of speaking. That doesn't mean that anything goes. We do learn conventions for expressing ourselves in even the most casual conversations. For less casual conversations, even if we think through what we are going to say and how we would like to say it, the expectation is less formal than it would be if we are reading a prepared statement. We expect some spontaneity from conversation, and we do not expect it to be governed by an overly formal agenda.

Second, *conversation is an interchange*, meaning that there is back-and-forth, give-and-take, movement from one person to another person—what is called turn-taking. We've all been in situations where conversation is stifled because one or more persons dominate, while the others fall silent, or where those involved seem to be speaking only to hear themselves rather than linking what they have to say to what others have said. Neither of these is genuine conversation because conversation is *between and among people*, rather than being a monologue or a sequence of statements ordered only by a change in who the speaker happens to be.

Third, *conversation occurs through the use of oral language*. Although "verbal" is often used to mean "oral" (as in "we had a verbal agreement"), the distinction between verbal and oral often gets lost. Verbal means "words" and can refer to both written and oral communication. "Oral" means spoken—saying something aloud.

Fourth, *conversation has diverse content.* Interchanges made possible through conversation might be of thoughts, information, and—to fill out the "etc." in the definition—opinions, directions, proposals, questions, answers. Sometimes we focus conversation on very specific content, and sometimes we let our interchanges roam free. The content distinctions are especially important when talking about complex matters such as race. In our technological era, we tend to refer to everything as "information," but that glosses over important distinctions. Information (and misinformation or lack of information) might lie in the background of perceptions, opinions, and biases. Information is often important to clarify things, but it's only one element of conversation. If, for example, I say that a comment someone made "was racist" or "wasn't racist," that's not information. It's my opinion and perspective on what was said.

Conversation offers several advantages for interpersonal understanding compared to other forms of communication. In addition to what is said (the oral component), face-to-face communication provides a broad range of nonverbal cues (facial expressions, gestures, body postures) that help us interpret what others are saying and how they are responding to the comments of others. Seeing someone nod in agreement or stiffen up in response to what has been said adds substantially to the meaning we interpret. Vocal aspects such as tone of voice, tempo, pitch, and intonation also shape what is said and how it is interpreted. The role and significance of nonverbal elements are substantial. Even for those with visual or hearing difficulties, nonverbal aspects of communication carry meaning. For a person who sees but does not hear clearly, gestures and facial expressions are magnified. For a person who hears but has compromised sight, tone of voice, tempo, pitch, and intonation will take on added importance.

Another advantage of conversation is that the informal back-and-forth nature of it allows us to modify what we've said. Although we cannot take back the words we utter or undo our facial expressions or tone of voice, we can retrace, modulate, and even dramatically change what we said a few minutes ago by saying something different. For example, you might state "a fact" that another person replies to with conflicting information or an alternate interpretation. You then might say, "I've never thought of that," "You're right," or "You seem to know more about this than I do." The point is that our statements, even though we cannot take them back, are not frozen in the way they are when we write them. We can clarify, change what we say, and add to prior statements.

To talk about race, then, involves more than making statements about the topic. To break our silences productively, we must learn to trust, to listen, to explore with others through respectful conversational interchange. These are mutual responsibilities, and there is no more important key to advancing understanding than the building of trust and respect for each other and each other's viewpoints. No one wants their experience denied or diminished. When that happens, the possibility for trust and respect diminish.

Why We Need to Talk about Race

What exactly makes talk about race an imperative for white people? There are many answers to that question, and the reasons why conversations about race are important will vary in priority from person to person. Here we offer five points as a framework for why it is important to talk about race.

1. We need to talk about race because racial thinking and racism undermine the common good. There's wisdom in the adage that "the whole is greater than the sum of its parts." If people of color are either not trusted—even if only because they are not known—or excluded, there is an enormous loss to the whole. There have been unjustified prejudices against many types of people over the years that have been exposed for the falsity of their claims—left-handers; those with physical disabilities; those of Irish, Japanese, and Jewish descent; and Native Americans. In each of those cases, changes in social attitudes have proven that the prejudice

was unfounded and served to disqualify or undermine those who differed from the norm or were perceived as a threat to the majority. The most enduring case of prejudice in the US has been the belief that people with black skin are less intelligent and less human than whites. The implication for the common good of sustaining that prejudice is to limit the potential in every facet of life by arbitrarily lopping off a section of the whole. Think of what it means to deprive the common good of contributions from over 13% of the US population because they are Black, or 18% because they are Latinx, or 6% because they are of Asian ancestry.[15] And think of the implications for any part that is excluded from the whole. The point is not that we are all the same but that we bring diverse perspectives and experiences to bear on every aspect of life. The greatest common good depends on the whole, and the greatest good for any part requires recognition of its worth and contributions to the whole.

2. We need to talk about race because people of different races tend to experience the day-to-day world in distinctive ways. More often than not, most of us know little about those distinctions and, even more important, why they exist. We can't improve racial understanding and race relations unless we confront and address what we think we know and where the gaps are in our understanding of other perspectives. It is often said that we learn from history. What that means is not that we aspire to repeat history, but that we draw new ideas and understanding from what happened in the past as a way of advancing. Similarly, knowing more about others can be both a corrective to our unquestioned beliefs and an addition to our understanding of how others conduct their daily lives; develop their ideas, tastes and beliefs; and build family and interpersonal relationships.

3. We need to talk about race because talk about race allows us to give voice to our thoughts and to ask questions. We

need to talk to help articulate and discover what we feel and think about race. In this sense, talk tests what we believe and why we believe it. Reciprocally, we need as part of true conversation to listen to others who give voice to their feelings and thoughts. We can begin with talking more purposefully with other white people—not only when we face a racially related "situation." We are not suggesting that talking about race with other white people will be easy or tension-free. Disagreements and disparate points of view will arise, as will the temptation to edit comments that we feel might be taken wrong or sound insensitive. But in same-race conversations, we won't be editing our comments for fear that a person of a different race will react badly or be evaluating our every word as a white person. We do, however, also need to talk across racial differences, to ask questions respectfully, to admit what we do not know, and to listen carefully without planning what we will say next.

4. We need to talk about race because conversation helps bring "white normalcy" and "white privilege" into consciousness. What is it that white people, just because we are white, *do not have to think about* that people of other races, just because they are not white, *do have to think about*? For example, do white people as a general group need to be concerned about surveillance when they enter a large store? Do white people as a general group have to worry that everything they do might be judged through a racial filter? Do white parents have to worry that their white sons who are old enough to drive will be followed by police just because they are white? In most cases, the answer to these questions is "no." Reverse the race, and the answer is "yes." Only through exploring exactly what white normalcy and privilege bestow on us can we begin to grasp the pervasiveness of discrimination and explore with others why we persist in approaching the world through white normalcy.

Some would contend that we can only know about the benefits of being white when people of color point out these benefits to us. There is definitely something to be gained from that. Yet, it is also true that we do not recognize these benefits because we do not have to focus on them so we take them for granted. Conscious thinking and focused observation about the benefits of being white can bring to our realization many taken-for-granted aspects of living our lives with "white as the norm." When we probe, we bring to our conscious awareness how race works to grant benefits. Both of us still often catch ourselves in the perspective of white normalcy when we might least expect it. As such, we experience a kind of protective barrier that is not available to people of color. What makes this not only embarrassing to us but also personally shocking is that both of us for many years taught and wrote about white privilege, and we parented Black children from infancy to adulthood. As part of a mixed-race family, we have learned to be aware of the racial composition of people wherever we go. But we still sometimes miss the obvious. For example, we participated in the 2018 Boston March for Our Lives to support gun control efforts of students from Marjory Stoneman Douglas High School in Parkland, Florida, after the shooting rampage at their school. We were well into the march before Fern saw a Black Lives Matter sign, prompting her realization that few Black people were marching. It simply didn't occur to her amid the throngs of people, the chanting voices, and the sea of posters. The "normalcy" of whiteness in our country is so deeply ingrained that unlearning it is never-ending and requires that we work together. We will say more about this in chapter 3.

5. We need to talk about race to air our feelings of guilt, embarrassment, and frustration. Embarrassment is a powerful blocker to conversation. It's often easier to push it aside

rather than to say, "I can't believe I just said/did that." Sometimes we feel reluctant to express views about race because we know they will sound racist to others or perhaps be racist. Even when whites talk with whites about race, there can be moments of embarrassment and guilt for what we express, and we can be called out for saying something that someone else finds racist. We need to learn to talk about race so that we can express what might make us feel embarrassed or guilty and talk it through with others.

In this chapter, we hope to have established the imperative for deep and probing talk about race. The imperative is a moral responsibility rooted in the need for greater social and economic justice. We know that some people who are reading this will say that they are tired of talk and it's time for action. We appreciate and often feel the same concern. But we believe that we cannot confront systemic racism and develop policies that will lead to racial equity until whites and Blacks are able to talk with each other about race. The fact that racism in the US appears more virulent today than it was several decades ago, that public schools in Boston are more segregated today than they were before busing in the 1970s, that reparations to the descendants of the enslaved is not only a divisive issue, it's also barely recognized as a legitimate issue by many whites—all speak to our inability to address racism at the macro level. We believe that the work must start at the micro level—with conversations that set the foundation for building understanding, trust, and the relationships necessary for us to work together to achieve racial equity. We need to start with talk because our words have consequences, and they can affect action. Our conversation, when thoughtfully developed, also helps us focus action more productively.

What's to Come

Chapters 2 to 5 lay out why it has been so difficult for white people to talk about race and what might help us move forward in our conversations. Each chapter explores one reason that it is difficult for whites to talk about race and to sustain conversations in a thoughtful, productive manner. We delve into the issues and sources involved for each specific topic. You will find "Personal Prompts" to stimulate your thinking and "Conversation Prompts" to focus conversations with white people and in cross-race situations. At the end of each chapter, we offer suggestions for how to approach the conversation, and for what we, as white people in this country, can do to improve racial understanding. These suggestions are organized into "dos" and "don'ts."

It is not our intention to guilt-trip whites or purposely touch a nerve that leads to defensiveness. We all start in different places, and each of us brings personal sensitivities and defensiveness to the topic of race. As authors of this book, the "we" absolutely includes us.

Chapter 2 provides context by considering the different forms of racism that exist in our society. Some have accumulated over a long period of time as sedimentary layers of history. Like literal sediment, we can't see down to the very bottom, but the bottom impacts everything above it. The more general forms of racism that we describe involve broad social and cultural practices, specifically *structural* and *institutional* sources of racism. Other forms of racism are more immediate and personal, specifically *individual, interpersonal,* and *internalized* racism. Unless we identify how these forms of racism work together to create a society where racial meaning is ever present one way or another, it will be difficult to move beyond racial talk that is stymied, superficial, and off-point.

Chapter 3 addresses white normalcy and white privilege. We explore the difficulties that many whites have in recognizing how important race is for personal experience and social identity. If we do not learn about, confront, and accept our white status, then we will continue in the erasure of race from our everyday consciousness. Our aim in this chapter is to reduce defensiveness about the idea of racial privilege and to open more channels for developing racial empathy.

Chapter 4 takes on the topic of white ignorance about the consequences of living in a racialized and often racist society. Ignorance is a conversation stopper as well as a powerful force in shaping what gets discussed. Whether structural or personal, the effects of racism need to be better known and understood—by both whites and people of color. For understandable reasons, most whites neither think about nor probe how race affects the key areas of society where "an even playing field" is supposed to be available. For that reason, we start chapter 4 with a sampling of historical information. The other areas covered in the chapter highlight four wide gaps between whites and people of color: unequal education, racialized patterns of health and health care, differential justice, and income inequality. Whites rarely grasp what it means to live day in and day out as a person of color marked for race. We don't know because our experience differs. We need to learn *how* to learn just as much as *what* to learn. Often this means unpacking generalizations, which will help us "get" *how* race changes experience. We might, for example, learn that the high school completion rate in the US is 90%. That's pretty high and represents steady improvement over the years. Yet, if we dig deeper, we learn that the rate is highest for non-Hispanic whites at 94%, lower for Blacks at 87%, and even lower for Hispanics at 71%.[16]

Chapter 5 looks specifically at cultural misunderstandings as an impediment to conversations about race. Because we live in a country that continues to carry the "melting pot" emblem either as a description or an attribution (remember *e pluribus unum*—"out of many one"), whites often assume that the way they do things is just the way it's done (white privilege and white normalcy). That assumption makes some cultural practices and preferences stand out as "odd," "exotic," or simply "interesting." At worst, the judgment is that they are "wrong" or "ignorant." It might be music identified as "Black," Aretha Franklin's funeral, Chinese Americans sending their children to Chinese school on Sundays, eating collard greens, or wearing hats in an age when hats are not the norm in the US. Sometimes when cultural practices differ, it's easy for whites to not recognize an important difference or to misinterpret the difference—because we have been the majority for so long. We might also be ignorant of why what a white person says about a Black person is offensive, for example, to describe a Black person as "articulate" or "well educated," thinking that these statements are

compliments. In the area of race relations, many cultural misunderstandings offend and propel mistrust. We as whites might make comments
that belie misunderstanding or are blatantly offensive. In this chapter,
we identify some of the sources of cultural misunderstanding through
concrete examples.

Chapter 6 brings together key points we have made throughout the
book and suggests ways to create safe spaces for conversations about
race. Our aim is not to draw cemented conclusions but rather to integrate ideas so that we have guidance for moving forward to build racial
understanding, trust, and relationships through productive conversations about race.

Chapter 2

Identifying Racism

Where Fiction Becomes Reality

T HE PURPOSE OF THIS BOOK is to help people, especially white people, talk about race. As a beginning, we focus in this chapter on the
concept of race, on several types of racism and racial thinking prevalent
in our society, and on how race can be better understood if we think
about its cultural context. Race, however, is a fiction, not a biological truism. Biological evidence does not support the concept of race.
Genetic data show that all humans descended from either a single population in Africa[1] or several populations across the continent that were
separated by environmental boundaries such as forests or deserts.[2] Over
thousands of years, people migrated to different parts of the world and
adapted physiologically to those new environments.

After years of studying purported racial differences, scientists have discovered greater biological variation within each race than between them,
which points to race as a category system based on something other than
biological differences. Scientists, however, do study small but important
differences among populations that are identified as races based on their
common geographic ancestry. For example, sickle cell disease is more prevalent among people of sub-Saharan African and Mediterranean ancestry,
cystic fibrosis and hemochromatosis are more prevalent among people of
European descent, and Tay-Sachs disease is more often found among
Ashkenazi (eastern and central European) Jews and French Canadians.

Overall scientists agree that racial categories are socially constructed,
created to explain, and in some instances, to justify economic and social

differences among groups. In 1998, the American Anthropological Association issued a statement on race, saying that "race as it is understood in the United States was a social mechanism invented during the 18th century to refer to those populations brought together in colonial America: the English and other European settlers, the conquered Indian peoples, and those peoples of Africa brought in to provide slave labor."[3] At its core, race is not about biology but about power.

The noted historian Jacqueline Jones argues that the use of race to justify slavery didn't come about until the American Revolution. Slavery has existed since ancient times, sometimes the result of one group of people conquering another group but always justified by slaveholders judging that those who were enslaved were economically, socially, or religiously inferior. Jones says that when enslaved people were first brought to America from Africa in 1619, slavery was the product of the "unique vulnerability of Africans within a roiling Atlantic world of empire-building and profit-seeking."[4] White settlers, therefore, had no need to justify enslaving Black people. They did it simply because they could, and it was economically profitable for them to do so. But when the American Revolution came along and elite whites began to fight for their own equality and liberty, arguing that "all men are created equal," they needed to rationalize the exclusion of Black men from the political life of the new nation. Thus, racial categories and their attendant hierarchies were born. Hitler employed the same technique in defining the Aryan race as superior to Jews, gypsies, homosexuals, and others. There is no Aryan race, but for Hitler it served brilliantly as a construction that was perpetuated by the Third Reich to justify the death camps.

If race is purely a social construction, why does it matter to us today? Thomas Chatterton Williams, a biracial writer, argues that people of color need to reject racial categories: "it is a mistake for any of us to reify something that is as demonstrably harmful as it is fictitious."[5] The difficulty with his argument, however, is that we have made race real for the entire history of the US, and in doing so, we have taken the fiction of race and created the reality of racism. And racism, although grounded in a fictional narrative, has substantive and material consequences for people of color.

Types of Racism

In this section, we provide a brief overview of the types of racism. Our overview barely scratches the surface of the subject. As with all the ideas in this book, we encourage you to read more deeply about racism.

Racism in the US ranges from the overt to the subtle and includes actions as disparate as the intentional or unintentional racial slur to the practice of redlining, in which banks charge higher interest rates for mortgages in communities of color. Most white people understand racism as something one person intentionally does to another (for example, shouting to a Black person to "go back to Africa," or calling a Chinese American "a China virus spreader"), but racism is much more extensive than individual acts of overtly racist people. Racism is divided into three categories: interpersonal, institutional (sometimes called structural), and internalized.

Interpersonal Racism

Interpersonal racism refers to the verbal or physical mistreatment of one person by another person because of the other's race or ethnicity. We have a long history of violence against Black people in the US. Although the 13th Amendment officially abolished slavery in 1865, it did not end violence by whites against Blacks. During the post-Civil War Reconstruction era, organized groups such as the Ku Klux Klan, the White League, and the Knights of the White Camelia engaged in the torture, lynching, and burning of Blacks. At that time, violence frequently erupted in communities when Blacks violated an expected norm, such as a Black man not tipping his hat to a white person he passed on the street.

The early part of the 20th century was marked by continued violence against Blacks, with stoning, lynching, and shooting of Blacks, especially in the South, along with the burning of entire communities. In 1921, the white citizens of Tulsa, Oklahoma, burned and looted homes and businesses in the Black section of north Tulsa. Estimates of the number of Blacks who were killed exceed 100, making it one of the worst race riots in US history. The middle of the century brought more violence as the civil rights movement led to desegregation and the integration of Blacks into daily life throughout the South.

Although racial violence is less frequent now, it is no less virulent when it occurs. Over the last few years, we have seen police killings of so many Black men and boys that it's hard to keep track of who they are and what happened in the aftermath of each case. And in June 2015, self-proclaimed white supremacist Dylann Roof went on a shooting rampage at the Mother Emanuel AME Church in Charleston, South Carolina, slaughtering nine African Americans during bible study. Some argue that mental illness drives killing more than anything else, but even when the assailant is clearly not psychologically "normal," the idea to kill Black people (or Jewish people, or Latinx people) has to come from somewhere in the culture.

In addition to violent racism, Blacks are likely to experience frequent verbal racism in both public and private. Blacks are often subjected to public verbal harassment. For example, in July 2012, a person sitting in the stands shouted "Monday" as Boston Red Sox player Carl Crawford walked onto the field. In this context, "Monday" is a euphemism for the N-word and refers to the belief that Monday is the least liked day of the week. The incident is especially telling because the person in the stands turned out to be a white police officer, an individual charged with protecting all citizens.

Many Blacks have experienced racist comments directed at them personally, in addition to the racist rhetoric in the larger public discourse. Although Mr. Trump engaged in verbal racism before becoming president, his racist comments from his candidacy through his years in office have been particularly virulent. He has characterized black and brown immigrants as rapists and terrorists, referred to African nations as "shit-hole" countries, and called for four women of color newly elected to the House of Representatives to go back to the "totally broken and crime infested places" that they came from, even though three of the four women were born in the US and all of them are, of course, US citizens. These few examples reveal the deeply ingrained cultural assumptions and stereotypes about people of color, now magnified and legitimized because they are uttered by the president.

Verbal racism isn't always intentional. Often negative attitudes toward and beliefs about racial groups based on stereotypes lead to racist comments. We remember when a grade-school teacher told us that one of our sons, who was struggling in school at the time, was "lazy." In fact, we knew he was working very hard, but the teacher's response was to label our son with the racial stereotype "Blacks are lazy." Much later we discovered he was having auditory processing problems related to hearing loss he experienced as a baby from repeated ear infections. Blacks, unfortunately, are accustomed to dealing with such comments because racial stereotypes are so deeply embedded in our culture that they are out of our awareness.

Personal Prompt: List as many stereotypes of African Americans that you can think of. Where did you first learn them? From your parents? From your friends? In your neighborhood? In school? In your place of worship? On television or in the movies? From other people or places?

Psychologists use the term "implicit bias" to describe stereotypes that unconsciously affect our attitudes, decisions, and behaviors. These stereotypes drive more than verbal racism. They provide the basis for unthinking actions or decisions that affect the lives of Black people. Whether it's the circulation of negative images of Blacks by mainstream media, a teacher's statement that a B grade is good enough for a Black child, or a manager's call to security to follow Black teens who are shopping in the store, implicit bias against Blacks is pervasive and dangerous.

A less obvious form of interpersonal racism is known as a *micro-aggression*. The term was coined in 1970 by Harvard psychiatrist Chester Pierce to refer to the daily insults endured by African Americans.

Conversation Prompt: In 2019, the National Football League (NFL) had 32 teams with 53 players on each team roster, for a total of 1,696 players. Of those players, 70% were Black. At the same time, there were 9 Black quarterbacks in the league, 3 Black head coaches, and 1 Black general manager. Discuss the possible reasons why there were so few Blacks in these positions.

Columbia University psychologist Derald Wing Sue has devoted substantial research to the topic. He defines *racial microaggressions* as "the brief and everyday slights, insults, indignities and denigrating messages sent to people of color by well-intentioned white people who are unaware of the hidden messages being communicated."[6] When a white person says to an African American, "You don't sound Black," that's a microaggression. The comment presumes that all Black people speak in the same way, and that it's surprising to hear a Black person speak what many call "standard" American English. When a white person crosses the street when they see a Black person walking toward them, they are signaling to that person that they believe Black people are dangerous. Microaggressions are commonplace and often never noticed by most white people. But they are noticed by people of color. And their constant assault has serious psychological and physical consequences. Ijeoma Oluo, author of *So You Want to Talk About Race*, recalls being aware of microaggressions such as comments about her big hair, big butt, or big lips as early as middle school: "I would be having a good day, lost in my imagination, and bam—I'd be hit with a comment that would remind me that I was not allowed to get comfortable."[7] She concludes that studies show that people subjected to microaggressions are more likely to experience mental and physical symptoms of depression.

Historian and antiracist scholar Ibram X. Kendi rejects the use of the term microaggression, saying that he "detests" both parts of the word—"micro" and "aggression." Kendi says that "a persistent daily low hum of racial abuse is not minor" because it leads to "distress, anger, worry, depression, anxiety, pain, fatigue, and suicide."[8] His point is important. As single acts, microaggressions are small. As a constant part of a person's life, however, their impact is huge. From a person of color's perspective, microaggressions are misnamed because the term glosses over their abusive power. We believe, though, that the term is useful for white people precisely because it forces us to look at interpersonal racism not simply as a single act of physical or verbal aggression against a person of color but rather as the constant, daily, always present insults and stereotypes that are rarely, if ever, noticed by white people. Although many whites cannot identify with being subjected to a constant onslaught of negative messages, thinking about racism as something that is always present may help us better understand its consequences.

Institutional/Structural Racism

Institutional/Structural racism occurs when societal institutions (political, economic, or social) provide more advantages or resources to people of one race than another. There are significant and continuing disparities between whites and Blacks in the US that are the result of the long history of discrimination against Blacks, discrimination that has been codified in policies and procedures across numerous institutions. In 2019, white Americans had seven times the wealth of Black Americans, with median family wealth for whites at $171,000 and only $17,600 for Blacks.[9] Although wealth is accumulated as it is passed down through generations (we explore this concept in chapter 4), employment income is also an important contributor to wealth disparities. What a person earns over time factors heavily in whether or not they will accumulate wealth and be able to save money. Research by the Economic Policy Institute revealed that wage gaps between Blacks and whites were larger in 2018 than in 2000 for every level of educational attainment—that's regress rather than progress.[10] Only Blacks with college degrees and advanced degrees had higher wages in 2018 than in 2000, but even among this group, wage growth was slower than it was for comparably educated whites. There is no way of knowing what the impact of the coronavirus will be on the wage gap, but prospects look grim.

Health care is another area in which there are significant disparities between Blacks and whites. Centers for Disease Control data reveal that Blacks have significantly higher rates of diabetes and hypertension than whites, and their life expectancy is 3.5 years less.[11] The death toll from the coronavirus provides further evidence: in Michigan, Blacks are 14% of the population and 40% of the deaths; in Wisconsin, 7% of the population and 33% of the deaths; in Mississippi, 38% of the population and 61% of the deaths.[12]

Given that these disparities do not exist because dark-skinned people are biologically inferior to light-skinned people, they must be the result of other factors. Those factors are primarily the result of institutional racism following from the legacy of slavery and discrimination. That legacy directly affects the quality of life for African Americans today.

Looking more closely at wealth disparities reveals the impact of institutional racism. Wealth disparities trace back to the institution of slavery. Enslaved Blacks were not paid for their labor and, therefore, had no wealth to accumulate. In the period immediately after the Civil War, Blacks initially thought they would have economic opportunities. In 1865, Union Army General William Sherman reallocated 400,000 acres of former enslavers' land along the coast of South Carolina, Georgia, and Florida. The plan became known as "40 acres and a mule." The promise of a better economic future, however, was short-lived. After President Lincoln was assassinated, Andrew Johnson pardoned white plantation owners and gave them back the land that had been allocated to Black families. Blacks made some economic progress during Reconstruction, but it was almost entirely wiped out during the racial violence against Blacks that erupted during the late 1800s and early 1900s.

Through much of the first half of the 20th century, numerous economic policies precluded Blacks from accumulating wealth: Jim Crow laws in the South stripped Blacks of their property; restrictive covenants precluded them from buying houses in white neighborhoods;

redlining by banks made mortgages for properties in Black neighborhoods prohibitively expensive; and discrimination in the application
of the G.I. Bill and other federal policies kept Blacks from gaining
access to free education and low-rate mortgages, advantages that allowed the growth of a vibrant middle class for whites in the US after
World War II.[13] Over time, home ownership drives the accumulation
of wealth. Whites who owned their own homes could live in good
neighborhoods and send their children to good schools. They had the
money to finance a college education for their children or to pay for
college outright, which was then much more affordable. Their children
had access to better-paying jobs, thus creating a self-perpetuating cycle
of upward mobility and wealth accumulation—part of the "American
dream." Professor Thomas Shapiro of Brandeis University, who has ex-
tensively studied the wealth gap in the US, concluded that "the wealth
gap is not just a story of merit and achievement, it's also a story of
the historical legacy of race in the United States."[14] Public policy professor William Darity, Jr. of Duke University and his colleagues echo
Shapiro: "We contend that the cause of the gap must be found in the
structural characteristics of the American economy, heavily infused at
every point with both an inheritance of racism and the ongoing authority of white supremacy."[15]

Conversation Prompt: In the previous prompt, we asked you to talk about
why there are so few Black quarterbacks, managers, and general managers
in the NFL. As of 2019, there were no Black owners of NFL teams. Discuss
why you think this is the case.

We examine structural racism more deeply in chapter 4, looking specifically at racial disparities in wealth and income, education,
health, and the criminal justice system. As you think about the types
of racism, keep in mind that while whites most often identify racism
as interpersonal, Blacks are more likely to be talking about structural

racism. Whites will likely see a police officer shoot a Black man and ask whether the officer was racist or justified in reacting as they did. Blacks will likely see the same event as one part of a criminal justice system that is stacked against Blacks, starting with the stereotype that Blacks, especially Black men, are more dangerous and more violent than whites. It's not surprising, therefore, that a 2016 Pew Research Center survey found that 75% of white respondents said that the police do a good or excellent job using the right amount of force when making an arrest as compared with only 33% of African American respondents.[16] Often when a Black person accuses a white person of being racist, the accusation is not directed at the individual, but rather at the person's participation, knowingly or unknowingly, in a racist system. As we show in our examination of structural racism in chapter 4, we are all complicit in that system.

Internalized Racism

Internalized racism occurs when individuals begin to believe prejudiced ideas about themselves or others who share their race or ethnicity. It "gives rise to patterns of thinking, feeling, and behaving that result in discriminating, minimizing, criticizing, finding fault, invalidating, and hating oneself while simultaneously valuing the dominant culture."[17] Perhaps the best-known example of internalized racism was seen in the studies done by Kenneth and Mamie Clark in the 1940s.[18] The Clarks, who were African American psychologists, showed Black children two dolls, one white and one black, and asked the children questions about them. The majority said that the white doll was nicer than the black doll and they would rather play with the white doll. Further, 44% of the children said that the white doll looked more like them than the black doll did.

More recently, the ABC television show, *Good Morning America*, conducted a similar experiment and found that 88% of the children identified with the black doll, 42% wanted to play with the black doll (only 32% preferred to play with the white doll, and the remaining 26% had no preference), and the majority said that either the black doll was nicer or there was no difference between the black and white dolls.[19] More than 70 years later, however, signs of internalized racism still appeared. When asked which doll was more beautiful, 47% of the girls identified the white doll. Looking more closely, we see further signs of internalized racism. For example, one child said the white doll was nicer because the black doll "talks back and don't follow directions" and another said the black doll was ugly because "sometimes this one has its feet like a monkey."

Today internalized racism might be expressed within communities of color in a variety of ways that tend to be invisible to whites—in low self-esteem, stereotyping, self-hatred, and color prejudice, for example. Whites are often surprised to learn that lighter-skinned Blacks are held in higher esteem than darker-skinned Blacks in many communities of color. Some color prejudice in these communities comes from the recognition that lighter-skinned people are more likely to be accepted by whites, but some of that prejudice is the result of having internalized white beliefs about the inferiority of dark-skinned people.

Donna Bivens, an anti-racism activist, reminds us that internalized racism should not be looked at as a personal issue or interpersonal problem. Instead, she argues that "there is a system in place that reinforces the power and expands the privilege of white people,"[20] and that people of color and communities of color are rewarded for supporting white privilege and power. Bivens identifies four ways that internalized racism manifests in the inner lives of African Americans: (1) having a sense of inferiority, (2) being grounded in victimhood, (3) being overwhelmed by emotions created by this identity of inferiority and victimhood, and (4) focusing on trying to figure out and change white people. These feelings lead to serious interpersonal, institutional, and cultural consequences. For example, Blacks may express rage at whites or project their sense of inferiority on other Blacks and, therefore, lack confidence in their leadership. In policy decisions, Blacks may defer to whites in positions of power, believing that they know better what Blacks need. Culturally, internalized racism may lead to cross-racial hostility, in which one oppressed group supports the oppression of another oppressed group. Each of these examples points to how internalized racism supports white power.

Racially Identified Cultures

Although race is socially constructed, the shared experiences of people of color in the US have led to the creation of *racially identified cultures.* Generations of African Americans have passed down a unique set of cultural practices and characteristics, including language, art, music, religious practice, literature, and modes of being and behaving. Over the long stretch of time since the beginning of enslavement, those characteristics have blended African ways of understanding and being with the experience of being Black in the United States.

We don't mean to suggest that African American culture and mainstream American culture are entirely separate entities or that all African Americans and all white Americans are culturally homogeneous. From music to fashion to hairstyles, Black Americans have helped to shape the cultural lives of all Americans and the perception by other cultures of what is uniquely American. For example, many musicians throughout the world recognize jazz, a creation of African American culture, as the quintessential American musical form. And while many whites appreciate and play jazz, many Blacks prefer other musical forms. Culture is complex. We start with a definition to help us understand the concept of culture and unpack its complexities.

Culture is the "patterned ways of thinking, acting, feeling, and interpreting" of particular groups.[21] Culture guides our understanding and behavior, and shapes how we approach the world. Culture can be national, regional, ethnic, racially based, religious, or generational, with any of these functioning in combination. Consider the example of national culture that writer Eva Hoffman gave in her autobiography, *Lost in Translation: A Life in a New Language.*[22] Of Jewish heritage, Hoffman was born in Krakow, Poland. Her family emigrated to Canada in 1959 when she was thirteen years old. She recounted passing around a journal to her classmates to "write appropriate words of goodbye" when she left Poland. Their words were sad and melancholy, creating a vision of life "as a vale of tears or a river of suffering." Two years later, she spent a month traveling with a group of American teenagers. When they said goodbye, she again passed around a journal for them to sign. Their messages were bright and cheerful: "It was great fun knowing you! Don't ever lose your friendly personality!" She compared the journals and concluded that she had "indeed come to another country." She had, in fact, entered another culture.

The workings of any culture are a mixture of different systems of meaning: *abstractions*, e.g., values, morals, ethics, logic, religious beliefs; *language and communication*; and *artifacts*, e.g., music, art, clothing, literature, rituals. Five aspects of culture help us understand what's going on below the surface.[23]

First, culture is not monolithic. The cultural patterns and practices we discuss do not apply to every person who might be identified with a certain label, such as African American or Italian American. We are all unique individuals with personal history and personality.

Second, culture is both passed down from generation to generation and ever-changing. What is passed down is not frozen. It reshapes over time and with evolving experience. Clothing is an example. Boys and girls are taught what it means to "dress up," but the ingredients for "dressing up" vary over time. Both of us are old enough to remember wearing gloves for dressy occasions, but that rarely occurs today. For men, the required suit, white shirt, and tie has given way in many contexts to the sport jacket and pants, shirt without tie, and so forth. We coin new terms such as "casual Fridays," "dress down," and "dress sneakers." It's not just style. It's culture on the move, with "style" a name for cultural practice.

Third, individuals possess tacit (implicit) knowledge of the cultural systems that underlie their everyday communication and action. Our cultural practices become so ingrained that we rarely think of them explicitly. There is truth to the idea that we "do what comes naturally," even though everything we do has been learned in one way or another. Think about the handshake as a greeting ritual. Before the coronavirus, we didn't think much about it; it was tacit knowledge. That's no longer true, and we are still learning new behavior.

Fourth, although cultural knowledge is tacit, members of groups that have been marginalized, discriminated against, or otherwise subjected to prejudice and bigotry possess more explicit awareness of their own and dominant cultural patterns than do the groups that are in control. For decades, Blacks in the US have adapted to the expectations of their white employers and teachers, with young children, for example, learning to maintain eye contact with teachers even though they may have been taught that direct eye contact with adults signals defiance, and with adults at work moderating the brightly colored clothing and hair style that they might prefer.

Fifth, cultures influence one another. This occurs most noticeably in multicultural societies where people mingle and media circulate images and narratives. Sometimes cultural practices merge to produce a new form. At other times, a practice is borrowed and placed into another cultural context. Some commentators on culture refer to this kind of borrowing as "cultural appropriation." Judgments of whether a cultural practice shows merging or borrowing and whether it evokes praise or scorn often resides in the interpreter. From Princess Diana to Meghan Markle, the royal wives have worn traditional Indian and Pakistani clothing; historically, they enjoyed praise for doing so. In recent years, however, some fashion commentators have complained about Western designers "appropriating" African and Asian styles.

Conversation Prompt: One of the most popular songs of 2019 was *Old Town Road* by Black rapper, Lil Nas X. The song debuted at No. 19 on Billboard's Hot Country Track after country music DJs picked it up off YouTube. Shortly after, Billboard removed the song from the Hot Country Track, saying "it doesn't embrace enough elements of today's country music." Some music critics said Billboard's decision was racist. Others agreed with the decision. Watch the YouTube video and discuss both points of view. Do you think the song was removed because Lil Nas X was a Black rapper or because the song wasn't really a country song?

Cultural influence is complicated. For example, what about a white rapper? Is that rapper (especially in the early days of rap music) participating in the ongoing music culture or borrowing and appropriating rap for their own purposes? Or a white woman greeting a Black woman she knows at work with "Hey girlfriend!" Is she simply catching a phrase that shows up in popular culture, or is this a microaggression because it's a greeting among Black women that shows solidarity? It depends on who the people are, where they are, and their relationship.

We look to culture to help us understand people but not to reduce individuals to the characteristics of that culture. We need to get to know Black people as individuals.

Most whites, in fact, know very little about African American culture and experience, primarily because we live in racially divided neighborhoods and travel in different friendship circles. Whites often say that they have African American friends, but they usually mean that they have colleagues at work or one or two friends from school. Much less common are interracial friendships in which the friends talk about and experience together the intimate details of their lives. Even when they do have close interracial friendships, Blacks and whites rarely talk about how Blacks experience race. Marlene recalls a conversation in one of her classes in which a white woman said that her closest friend in high school was Black and that her friend never experienced racism in school. A Black woman in the class raised her hand and said to the white woman, "Did you ever ask her if she did?" Not surprisingly, the answer was "No."

Professor Marsha Houston, who is African American, studied communication between Black and white women and described their conversations as "difficult dialogues" because white women and Black women have different expectations about conversation that lead them to assess the talk of the other negatively.[24] Houston elaborates on this by saying that white women believe Black women don't speak with proper grammar, diction, and decorum, and Black women believe white women talk around issues, avoiding conflict and not saying what they mean. The lack of understanding, she concludes, leads white women to assume that Black women are inferior and Black women to assume that white women are untrustworthy. These differences in conversational expectations are an example of cultural differences.

Another reason that most whites know little about African American life is because they have *white privilege*, defined by white anti-racism activist Peggy McIntosh as "an invisible package of unearned assets."[25] Whites in America can be in the company of people of the same race whenever we choose, can turn on the television or go to the movies and see white people on the screen, and when we buy bandages can be assured that they will match the color of our skin. Whites also don't have to worry about "stop and frisk" police policies, "driving while Black," "shopping while Black," or even just "living while Black." Perhaps our most significant privilege is not having to know *in every situation and every day of our lives* anything about people who are not white, because being white is the norm.

We explore both white privilege and the separation of whites and Blacks in greater depth in subsequent chapters and devote chapter 5 to an examination of cultural misunderstandings that might arise between whites and Blacks.

Personal Prompt: African American author Ta-Nehisi Coates, writing about President Barak Obama, said that Obama trusted white people and believed they wouldn't discriminate against him because, having been raised by a white mother and white grandparents, "The first white people he ever knew, the ones who raised him, were decent in a way that very few Black people of the era experienced."[26] Think about your first experiences with Black people. What did you learn from them?

Moving the Conversation Forward
Things Not to Do

- Knowing that race is socially constructed and not biologically determined, and that racial discrimination is wrong, does not mean that whites should say "I don't see color." We all "see" color, even those who are genetically color-blind. Children as young as three years old will comment on the color of their own and others' skin. Racism shapes the experience of people of color. To say to a Black person that you don't see their color is to erase their experience. You can acknowledge racial differences and, more importantly, differences in experiences and ways of looking at the world, without buying into race as a biological category.

- Don't say "I'm Jewish" or "I grew up poor" so I understand your experience as a Black person. Everyone who is a member of a marginalized group or has experienced hardships understands the experience of being an outsider or of having fewer privileges than others. But the experiences of each group are unique. As a white person, to say that you understand what it's like to be Black because you've experienced discrimination and hardship erases the experience of Black people. We don't know what it's like to be Black. That's why many African Americans were offended when Democratic presidential candidate Pete Buttigieg said, "I am gay, so I understand." We can't experience life as a Black person, but we can try to develop empathy for that experience, and we can draw on our own experiences as members of groups who have been discriminated against to help us develop that empathy.

Things to Do

- Try to focus more on the feelings of others and less on your own. As we said earlier, one way that internalized racism manifests for African Americans is in their focusing on "reading" and trying to change white people. Doing that places an unfair burden on them to maintain conversations through their attention to both the verbal content—often having to "teach" whites about the world that Blacks experience—and the nonverbal content—constantly taking the emotional temperature of the whites in the conversation. White self-defensiveness is often a response that comes from feeling that "I'm not a racist." White people need to check their self-defensiveness when talking about race and to work on taking responsibility for our own learning. We white people need to be more generous—to think less about our emotional responses in conversations about race and more about the emotions that people of color may be experiencing. We don't expect that whites, who have historically been centered in discourse, can immediately shift to the margins, but it's crucial that we begin to shift the burden of care so that everyone in the conversation shares that responsibility.

• Another way to shift the burden of care is to speak up when you hear a white person use a microaggression or say or do something that may be racist. But be careful not to speak for a person of color. White people need to negotiate a very fine line between supporting Blacks and perpetuating white privilege by speaking for them. We recently participated in a community book discussion about race. The young Black woman facilitating the conversation opened with an emotional statement about how racism causes her to wake up in pain every day. At one point, she said that she often noticed nonverbal cues from white people in town that she experienced as hostile. A white woman in the group interrupted her to ask what those cues were because, as she said, "I don't want to do that to you." Another white woman pounced on her declaring, "You interrupted. That's what white people do all the time—interrupt Black people. I don't want to hear from you. I want to hear from Susan [name changed] not you." Susan then said she didn't mind the interruption because she wanted to answer the question. The white woman who called out the original interruption was correct in saying that this is what whites often do in conversation with people of color. Her lengthy and angry comments, however, allowed her to become the center of the conversation—exactly what she accused the other woman of doing. Speak up, but don't speak for others.

- When you or someone else describes or responds to the description of a racist act by an individual, try to tie that individual act to systemic racism. Ijeoma Oluo says that linking an act of individual racism to its systemic consequences helps white people recognize systemic racism and understand how racism differs from other forms of prejudice.[27] For example, if you are a white teacher and you hear another white teacher shout at a Black middle-school boy who is acting up in class and being rowdy, "You're going to end up in jail if you keep this up," don't just say the act was racist. After you tell the teacher that the comment was racist, explain that the beliefs and attitudes about Black children that underlie the comment are linked to the higher rates of suspension and expulsion from school that Black children experience. This explanation should help the teacher understand that statements that are racist have consequences beyond the words themselves. Or when a white person in a conversation about the N-word says, "I've been called a 'cracker' and that's the same," ask the person if they have been denied employment or housing because of their identity as a "cracker."

Together, these dos and don'ts are just a beginning, as are the ideas presented in this chapter. Readers will have their own ideas for how to improve our thinking and conversations about race based on their own personal experiences. As white people, we need to get more knowledge and understanding about race into our heads, and we need also to get out of our own heads to listen to what others have to say. Doing both will expand every person's list of dos and don'ts to move conversation in a more positive direction.

Chapter 3

Erasing Our Race

Normalizing and Privileging Whiteness

TALKING ABOUT RACE IS DIFFICULT. As we said in chapter 1, sustained calls for a national conversation about race have gone unanswered even as racial violence has escalated. One news story after another details the killings and questions whether justice prevails. Even past incidents reemerge. Four years after her death, the cell phone recording Sandra Bland made when she was stopped by a police officer for a minor traffic violation was released to the public. We had seen and heard the police video, but the video from Bland's camera gives us a close-up image of the state trooper, his face contorted in anger, pulling out a stun gun and shouting "I'm going to light you up." The video undercuts the trooper's claim that he feared for his life.

That racism is alive and well in the US is clear with even a cursory glance at the daily news. In addition to the continuing incidents of police brutality directed primarily at Black men, we read about racist graffiti and online taunts, racial incidents at schools, and ongoing racial disparities throughout society. To the repertoire of "driving while Black" and "shopping while Black," we now have #Living While Black. This hashtag identifies the many ways that white people "police" Blacks by calling the police whenever they see Blacks in places whites believe they don't belong or engaging in behaviors whites don't like, at least not when Black people engage in them. With racism deeply entrenched in the culture, why can't we talk about it?

Being White

There are many reasons why whites, regardless of political leanings, can't talk about race, but a major one is that we don't see ourselves as having a race. When we talk about race, we do not include ourselves in the conversation. Most whites in the US live in predominantly white communities or enclaves within more diverse cities and towns. The separation of the races is further amplified when we look at friendship patterns. Reporting on a 2014 study, reporter Christopher Ingraham commented, "Blacks have ten times as many black friends as white friends. But white Americans have an astonishing *91 times as many* white friends as black friends."[1] For whites in the US, being white is the norm. We see the world through the lens of whiteness without acknowledging that whiteness—unless, of course, we find ourselves in a situation where we are the sole white person or one of only a few.

Personal Prompt: (1) Name your 20 closest friends. (2) If you were planning to host a party this weekend, name the 20 people you would invite. (3) Think back to a family event you've hosted such as a graduation party, wedding, bar or bat mitzvah, baby shower, etc. Who were the people who attended? What do your responses tell you about your friendship circle?

White Privilege

As we said in chapter 2, whites carry with them invisible assets which Peggy McIntosh calls white privilege. The privileges of being white are many. Several years ago, a Black colleague of ours told us about when her adolescent daughter came home from her ballet lesson and said that her teacher asked the students to purchase flesh-colored tights for their upcoming recital. She scoured the local shops looking for brown tights that matched her daughter's skin. When her daughter arrived for the recital, the teacher was aghast to see the dark tights. Flesh-colored meant the "flesh" color of white skin. Our colleague was embarrassed for her daughter and outraged that the teacher had been so thoughtless in requesting flesh-colored tights without clarifying whose flesh she meant. But the teacher's thoughtlessness is exactly what white privilege is all about—never having to think about your race, unless you're in a crowd of people of color.

Whites never have to think about race because one of the most powerful assets we carry with us is the normalization of whiteness. Being white is the default against which we measure everyone. In her novel *Little Fires Everywhere*, Celeste Ng tells the story of a Chinese infant, abandoned by her single mother and fostered by a white family desperate to have a child of their own. Shortly before the adoption becomes final, the birth mother asks for her return. The community is divided over who should have the child. Her white foster mother is interviewed for local television and asked if the baby has any dolls. She responds, "Of course. Too many." The interviewer then asks, "What do they look like?" She responds that most of them have blond hair and the one whose eyes close has blue eyes. She then says, "But that doesn't mean anything. You look at the toy aisle—most dolls are blond with blue eyes. I mean, that's just the *default* [emphasis ours]."[2] Yes, dolls of color can be found, but not everywhere and not always easily. Unlike white dolls which are "just there," black dolls are placed in market niches that have potential Black consumers.

That "default" is how we define the world around us. Mainstream American standards of beauty are white—blonde, silky, straight hair; blue eyes; narrow nose; slender body. Notice how many white women with dark hair color it lighter, rather than the reverse. Standards for public behavior, even taking regional and ethnic differences into account, are the creation of white people—decorum and moderation lest a person be described negatively or in some ethnic manner. Our acceptable language and communication patterns are white—standard-sounding English spoken with "correct" grammar.

No doubt many whites don't measure well against all these standards. But the standards aren't there to measure whites. They exist to measure those who are different. And because we measure people of other races against whiteness, they, by definition, fall short. They are deficient simply because they are not white.

The normalization of whiteness also means that we think about whiteness as typical, as usual, in other words, as normal. White people usually don't "see" the experiences of people of color because we assume that how we experience the world is the only way it can be experienced. And when people of color tell us that their experiences differ, it's easy for a white person to deny those experiences or see them as personal to the individual. You might be thinking that you know many white people who differ from you in various ways. That's true. There are substantial differences in personality, style and taste, parenting, and so forth. But for us white people, there is always a blanket of commonality that covers those differences and can exclude the experiences and perceptions of others by judging them to be outside the norm. A Black participant in a race dialogue that Marlene was facilitating shared a long story about taking a family member to the hospital the previous weekend. He said that the family waited a long time for assistance, and when the ill person was finally seen by a doctor, the other family members were taken to a waiting area and left without any follow-up information for many hours. He attributed their treatment by the medical staff to the fact that the family was Black. When the man finished telling his story, a white woman in the group quickly raised her hand and said that she was a nurse and could absolutely assure him that anyone would have been treated in the same way at that hospital and that race was not the reason. The Black man listened patiently and then quietly said, "You are denying my experience. You don't have any way of knowing how I and my family are treated in public places." The issue is not whether race was the cause of the treatment. The issue is the white woman's refusal to consider that a Black man's experience might be racially based and, therefore, different from hers. As a nurse, the white woman may also have felt that she needed to defend people in the medical profession as not racist. Again, however, her defense simply denies the Black man's experience.

As college professors who taught many courses that introduced students to the concept of white privilege, we assumed we were savvy about what white privilege means in real life. It was only after we adopted a Black child that we came to see our privilege. When we were out with our son, people (white and Black) would come up to us and almost tearfully tell us what wonderful people we were and how bless-ed our son was because we had adopted him. Would they have said the same if we were two Black women with a white baby? We doubted that. Many years later, a Black friend recounted how, when she was out with her light-skinned child, she was mistaken for his nanny. White privilege is a form of internalized white supremacy. We deny that we have a race while, at the same time, we tacitly "see" our race as supe-rior. We recognize that white supremacy is a term that is fraught for many whites and often leads to defensiveness and even anger. It is also, however, a term that captures what it means when a person or group sees and/or benefits from their way of living in the world because of its "normalcy" and, by implication, its being better than other ways of living in the world. The *Cambridge Dictionary* defines *supremacy* as "the leading or controlling position," "position of being the best," and "the highest authority or greatest power." As such, the word accurately describes how we normalize and privilege whiteness.

The dangers of white privilege are many, but perhaps the most se-rious one is how it prevents whites from being able to understand the daily burdens that Blacks carry with them. Many years ago, when our children were very young, we stopped to look at a beach house for rent on Cape Cod. The owner assured us that the house was available. We told her that we had a few other houses to look at and we would call her early the next morning to let her know if we wanted the house. When we called, she said that the house was no longer available. Hearing that, we were convinced that she would not rent to us because our children were Black. The owner proved us wrong a few hours later when she called back to say that she had convinced the people who had rented the house to change their rental dates because she thought our boys were adorable and would love staying in her house. The damage was done, however, because the moment we heard that the house was no longer available to rent, we understood the horror of believing that everything that happens to you might be because of your skin color. We also understood how that belief would constantly haunt us and would sometimes even distort our understanding of events in our lives and our children's lives. Why didn't he get a solo in the band concert? Why was he left out of the team photograph? We even questioned the good things that happened, thinking that the boys sometimes received good grades or accolades simply because they were Black and other people either had low expectations for them, or were afraid to judge them fairly for fear of being called racist. We weren't always right about why things happened, but often we were. That meant we had to be constantly vigilant.

The daily burden of being Black in America is further intensified by the responsibility to represent the race. McIntosh identified one of the privileges of whiteness as the ability to assume that both the good and bad things that happen to you are not attributed to your race. Blacks, on the other hand, always represent their race—positively or negatively. When you don't succeed, it's proof that your race is inferior, either inherently or because of the limitations of your experience and opportunities. When you do succeed, it's because you were given special consideration or you are exceptional. Your strengths and weaknesses are never your own. In an interview on NPR's *Story Corps*, Charisse Spencer, a Black woman who as a youngster helped integrate an all-white school in the 1950s, recalled that despite having to walk several miles to and from the school each day and enduring verbal and physical abuse from white children, she succeeded: "We all did really good at that school. We had to. We were representing our whole race."[3]

Understanding white privilege is essential for an honest discussion about race. But the concept and naming it "privilege" are fraught for many whites. Thus, when white privilege is introduced into a discussion about race, many whites shut down, sometimes because they feel enormous guilt about having privilege and sometimes because they don't see their white privilege, which is often masked by the absence of privilege in other aspects of their lives, for example, social class, economic status, sexual orientation, or religion.

Seeing White Privilege

A brief examination of Marlene's early life reveals how difficult it often is for many whites to see white privilege. Marlene, who is Jewish, grew up in a small town in New Jersey that was predominantly Catholic. Her parents had little money. When she was a child, her father worked three jobs to make ends meet for the family. He rode a bicycle to work every day—in the rain, snow, sleet, blinding heat. He bought his first car when she was eight years old. Discrimination against Jews was very real when Marlene was growing up. On Easter Sunday each year, the Catholic priest reminded worshippers that the Jews killed Christ, and the children in church who heard the sermon chased the Jewish kids home from school the next week, shouting "You killed Christ." To this day, when Marlene tells this story, she knows it's likely that a non-Jewish person might not believe this happened.

As far back as Marlene can remember, she recalls discrimination. In the early 1950s, at the height of McCarthyism, Jews were often singled out and accused of being Communist sympathizers. Several friends of Marlene's parents lost their jobs at a local army base. Marlene remembers that, when she was in high school, the best paying summer job for girls was working for AT&T, but the company didn't hire Jews. Marlene was the first in her family to go to college and had her heart set on attending a private college, but her family could afford only a public university. When she moved into her dormitory, a student she met there said, "I thought all Jews had horns." When her organic chemistry professor scheduled the first exam on Yom Kippur, he told the Jewish students who asked for a make-up exam that he would reluctantly write one but none of them would pass it. None of them did.

Because Marlene came from a working-class family that experienced anti-Semitism, she never thought that she had any kind of privilege. But she did have white privilege because she could move about without being seen as racially different.

In workshops and classes, both of us have included an exercise called the "Opportunity Walk" or "Challenge Walk," which is based on examples of white privilege. Participants, who always include people of different races, line up shoulder to shoulder across an open space. They are asked to take a step forward or backward in response to forty questions about their experiences, both as children and now. (The exercise has been adapted by many trainers and the number of questions may vary; some readers may know the exercise.) For example, if your ancestors were enslaved in this country or elsewhere, take a step back. If you felt welcome in any neighborhood you visited when you picked your current apartment or house, take a step forward. At the end of the exercise, we ask people to look around and see where they are standing relative to others in the group. Invariably, those participants at the front of the line are white and those at the back are Black. The middle group is mixed.

The exercise is very powerful, and participants often become emotional as they "see" where they are in the group. Blacks are rarely surprised that they are at the back. Whites, on the other hand, are often surprised they are at the front, especially those who identify as not having privilege in some aspect, or even multiple aspects, of their lives. For some whites, the exercise is an eye-opener, allowing them to see white privilege and its effects. It's especially powerful in helping whites understand, in a personal and direct way, how institutional and systemic racism unfairly advantage whites and disadvantage people of color.

For Marlene, the exercise helped her see her white privilege. Growing up, she saw her family as financially less well-off than her peers in school. Although her parents had little money, her mother's mother had saved enough to lend her parents the down payment on a small house in New Jersey, and the GI Bill afforded her father the opportunity to get a low-cost mortgage to cover the rest. A few years later, her parents wanted to move to a town with a better school system. They combined the proceeds from the sale of their house with a small inheritance from her father's family to make the down payment. A young Black family would not have had the same opportunity.

Although Black GIs were technically eligible for the same government guaranteed housing loans that Marlene's father received, banks generally wouldn't make mortgage loans to Blacks for homes in Black neighborhoods. Blacks also were often excluded from white suburbs by restrictive deed covenants, which became common when the Supreme Court validated their use in 1926 in *Corrigan v. Buckley*. By 1940, 80% of property in Chicago and Los Angeles carried restrictive covenants.[4] Informal racism also kept Blacks out of white suburbs. Fern remembers as a young child hearing her parents talk about her father attending a meeting of other homeowners on the block to discuss the Black family who recently moved into the neighborhood. Not long after the meeting, the Black family moved out. When she asked why they moved, she was told that "they would be happier living someplace else." Marlene remembers a similar experience.

Lack of access to mortgages did more than preclude Black families from owning their own homes. Home ownership comes with a wealth (pun intended) of benefits. In the post-World War II era, homes generally increased in value, creating household wealth that could be used to finance college educations for children and later be passed down to those same children to help them acquire more wealth. Researchers who have studied the current wealth gap between whites and Blacks conclude: "Over the longer term, wealth can expand the prospects of the next generation, helping to pay for college, provide a down payment for a first home, or capitalize a new business."[5] Even today, when prospects for generational advancement for white income and assets are less rosy, the legacy of decades of increasing assets remains. This is not the case for almost all Blacks and many other people of color.

Marlene also began to see other privileges she possessed simply because she was white. As the first person in her family to attend college, she knew little about what to expect when she arrived on campus. All along the way, however, faculty members took her under their wings and mentored her. Young women lecturers invited her to dinner and became her role models for how to dress, talk, and behave. Professors encouraged her to go to graduate school and even introduced her to faculty on the admissions committees of the schools she applied to. Marlene knew she was a good student—bright, hard-working, and engaged in numerous extra-curricular activities that brought her to the attention of people who could help her. She appreciated the help and support she received and never questioned why she received it. It was not until Marlene began to do racial equity work, that she understood that a Black woman in the same circumstances was unlikely to have received the same mentoring and support she had received.

There were very few students of color and even fewer faculty of color at the large universities that each of us attended. In fact, neither of us ever encountered a faculty member of color in college or graduate school. Research shows that white faculty members today are less likely to mentor students of color.[6] A young Black woman (or man) going to college when either of us did would be hard-pressed to find any faculty of color to serve as role models or mentors unless they attended a historically Black college. Yet research also shows that mentoring is enormously helpful for students negotiating college, especially for first-generation students.

Marlene's story reflects the privileges many whites in the US possess and yet have little to no understanding that they possess them. Accepting that privileges afforded whites undergirded Marlene's parents' ability to give their children a better life does not diminish their hard work. The privileges associated with being white did not, by themselves, allow her parents to accumulate the necessary wealth to move to a better school district and then send their children to college. Her father's work ethic and her mother's ability to save money were a critical part of their success. And Marlene didn't graduate from college, receive a doctorate, and later achieve a tenured faculty position simply on the strength of being white. But the fact that she is white gave her the opportunity to work hard and achieve those things.

Our discussion of white privilege is not intended to ignore or gloss over the experiences of whites who face enormous obstacles. We recognize that there are people who suffer from debilitating diseases or face physical and mental challenges. We know that some whites are born into poverty that is generational and virtually impossible to overcome. But whites in the worst of circumstances do not face the *additional burdens associated with being Black.* Instead, we always carry with us the privileges associated with being white without the extra disadvantage of being Black. In a conversation about race with us, a Jewish woman commented that the Nazis used the concept of race to mark Jews, gypsies, and others as inferior to justify their enslavement and slaughter. She went on to say, however, that here in the US, unlike in Nazi Germany where Jews were required to wear armbands with a Jewish star to mark their identity, her day-to-day experience differs from Blacks because when she leaves the synagogue, nothing marks her race. None of this means that anti-Semitism no longer exists. There's plenty of evidence that it does and that its expression has increased significantly in recent years. But most Jews in the US are white, meaning that they do not carry markers of racial difference with them everywhere they go.

Personal Prompt: Take the Opportunity Walk by yourself. You can find the questions at uh.edu/cdi/diversity_education/resources/activities/pdf/privilege-walk.pdf. The document includes instructions for how to use the exercise with a group, but you can try it by yourself. You'll start standing in the middle of a room or hallway. When you've finished answering the questions and taken your steps forward and back, look at where you are in the room and think about what your position means. Where do you think other people might be standing relative to you?

NOTE: You can do this exercise with a group if you have a group of people who have started to talk about race. Be aware, however, that the exercise taps into issues that are highly emotional. Many people find the exercise wrenching, often because they see their privilege or lack of it when they see where people are standing at the end of the exercise.

The Opportunity Walk helps some people understand why people of different races not only experience the world differently but also find it difficult to recognize that their experiences are different. People at the front of the line often comment that they are surprised to see who is behind them when they turn around. Many then realize that we usually don't turn around to see who is behind us, and we also usually don't understand that the experiences of those who are behind differ from ours. Why don't we see those behind us? Because we don't move through life with a rearview mirror. Instead we tend to focus on what is in front of us, which reinforces our perception that everyone is experiencing the world as we do. White privilege means never having to acknowledge those who are behind us.

White Guilt

Discussion doesn't always follow easily from exercises like the Opportunity Walk because some whites feel intense guilt when they realize the extent of their privilege. All too often, guilt over white privilege shuts down talk about race.

Another useful racial equity exercise is one in which whites and people of color move into separate spaces to talk about what makes them proud of their racial identity and what challenges they face because of that racial identity. The groups invariably respond quite differently to having to answer these questions.

We have found that white groups often begin by questioning the "wisdom" of separating whites and people of color. They say things such as "it makes me uncomfortable" that people of color are moving to a separate space or "why am I lumped together with other white people with whom I have nothing in common?" Those initial responses are not surprising. Because white people generally do not see themselves as having a race, they don't see commonalities based on race among themselves. Instead, they see other categories of commonality—ethnicity, religion, social class, education, hobbies. They are brought up short when they are told that Black people aren't alike either, but they are often segregated and assumed to be the same. The discomfort that some whites feel when they see people of color seemingly forced to sit together or moved into a separate space seems to come from a deep sense of guilt about how people of color were treated historically. When asked why they object to having people of color meet separately, whites sometimes say that it reminds them of segregation and the forced separation of Blacks and whites. They are often surprised when people of color respond that they don't mind moving into a separate group for the exercise. Another source of white discomfort is the suspicion that people of color are saying negative things about them.

After the groups are separated, each begins by discussing the first question, What makes you proud of your racial identity? Invariably, the white participants look at each other in silence, waiting for someone to offer an idea. Sometimes no one does, forcing a facilitator to step in and suggest something. The conversation remains stilted and relatively quiet, with whites either expressing the belief that they have nothing to be proud of or that they feel guilty that their achievements were at the expense of others. Sometimes a person will say that they envy people of color because they could name many things to be proud of. The irony of the statement is usually lost on the group. We're sure that there are whites in these groups that might disagree, but they feel pressured to remain silent. They don't believe that it's okay to be proud of being white in the context of a dialogue about race. Guilt and fear keep the conversation muted.

Conversation Prompt: Do this exercise with a group of white people. Make a list of the things that make you proud of being white. Then make a list of things that you find challenging about being white. Discuss the list.

In contrast, the discussions among people of color are lively and loud. There's a sense that people are breathing a sigh of relief as they move into a group without white people. They are eager to answer the questions, especially the first one. They have much to say about what makes them proud of their racial identity. Blacks often cite their resilience and strength in the face of enslavement and present-day discrimination; their deep spiritual commitment and faith; jazz, gospel,

blues, rap, Motown, and other "black" music; soul food such as bar-
becue, corn bread, collard greens, and other Southern specialties; their
playfulness and facility with language; their ability to have succeeded
in dance and sports despite the odds; the remarkable achievements
of Black women and men in many fields where they always had to
do so much better than their white counterparts. Latinx groups talk
about their love of "la familia"; their deep religious commitment to
Catholicism; their colorful clothing, lively music, spicy foods; their
strong interpersonal relationships and ethic of loyalty.

The groups of color also have much to say about the challenges they
face as members of their racial or ethnic group. Heads nod in agreement as people share stories of being stopped by the police or followed
by security guards in stores, mistaken for janitorial staff at work, or
yelled at by someone hurling a racial epithet. People listen closely and
validate each other's experiences.

When the groups come back together, whites remain uncertain
about why they were grouped together, often even after people of color
report back that they felt more comfortable talking to each other. The
differences in how the groups respond to the exercise point to some of
the reasons we've suggested that make it so difficult for white people to
talk about race—guilt, fear of saying something offensive or "politically incorrect," inability to see the experiences of others, denial of having
either a race or racial privilege, and defensiveness.

Being Black

Not having the privileges that whites enjoyed historically created
significant material disadvantages for Blacks. Blacks have higher unemployment rates, lower educational achievement, and lower wages
than whites, and overwhelmingly, they live in substantially lower-qual-
ity housing. As noted in chapter 2, the net result of these and other
material disadvantages is that Black wealth, including inherited wealth,
lags significantly behind white wealth. One study analyzed financial
transfers (monetary gifts, payment of bills, and inheritance) within Black
and white college-educated families from 1989 to 2015: 41% of white

families passed money to younger generations, compared to only 13% for Black families; and the average financial transfer for white families was $150,000 compared to $40,000 for Black families.[7] A 2015 study conducted by the Federal Reserve Bank of Boston, Duke University, and the New School found that the household median net worth of whites was $247,500, compared with $12,000 for Caribbean Blacks, and only $8 for African Americans. This astoundingly huge disparity led *Boston Globe* writer Akilah Johnson to say, "That was no typo."[8]

Not having privilege leads to other consequences that have serious ramifications for everyday life as a Black person in the US. For example, whites often accuse Blacks of "playing the race card" when they claim racism underlies their experiences. One of the privileges of being white is not having to represent our race in everything we do. We can be assured that what happens to us, good or bad, happens because of our own successes and failures, good or bad luck, or some other situational factor: we worked hard, we treated others with respect, we managed our money wisely, and so forth. Of course, the irony of this belief is that much of our success is the result of the powerful background of being white. As we said earlier, our experiences as the parents of Black sons taught us that we would see race as the issue in all situations, whether good things or bad things were happening to our children. Believing that race is the reason why things happen often leads to confrontations with white people. As one of Fern's Black colleagues once said, "Sometimes I'm right and sometimes I'm wrong, but I always have to name it because I'm right some of the time." Naming it all of the time knowing that they will be right some of the time means that Blacks may be perceived by whites as "playing the race card," which undermines trust between Blacks and whites.

Not having privilege also makes Blacks suspicious about the intentions of whites, and that suspicion makes it difficult to establish the trust necessary for genuine conversations about race. Rebecca Carroll, a cultural critic and author of several books on race, wrote a commentary on photographs of feminist icon Gloria Steinem that showed Steinem shoulder to shoulder with Black feminists throughout her career. In talking about Steinem, Carroll, who is Black, said, "I have struggled with trust in my interactions with white women.... So it is no small thing for me to say that Gloria Steinem...is among the very few I trust resolutely, instinctively and without conflict or concern."[9] Why? Because, Carroll says, Steinem listens to Black women. The point again is that Blacks often don't trust the intentions of whites.

Lack of privilege also makes Blacks fearful—fearful of being harassed either through overtly racist comments and actions or more subtly through microaggressions that well-meaning whites don't even recognize as hurtful. When our children were young, we had to teach them how to tell people that it wasn't appropriate to touch their hair without permission. Fast-forward to 2018 and Marlene's cardio swim class when the white instructor explained that the gym could no longer use "Zumba" in the name of the class because the licensed Zumba instructor was no longer working there. She suggested that the gym could now call the class "Ghetto Dance." She thought the name was cute, but Marlene was not alone in being appalled at her insensitivity. Similar comments, called dog whistles, have become commonplace in political life. A dog whistle is a coded message communicated through words or phrases commonly understood by one group of people but not others. When Ron DeSantis—a white man—was running for governor of Florida in 2018, he said "The last thing we need to do is to *monkey this up* [emphasis ours] by trying to embrace a socialist agenda with huge tax increases."[10] White voters in his base understood that he was referring to Andrew Gillum, his Black opponent.

Blacks are also fearful of being harassed while doing the ordinary activities of daily life—driving, shopping, even eating lunch. It's no wonder that many Blacks prefer not to engage with whites except when they must because they are in their workplaces, classrooms, or other public spaces.

White privilege does more than empower and privilege whites. By racially marking those who are not white and erasing the race of those of us who are white, white privilege establishes Blacks and other people of color as the "other," as those who are different. Ironically, just as white privilege erases whiteness as a racial category while simultaneously establishing the white race as superior, lack of privilege positions people of color on the margins, where they are unseen or ignored, while simultaneously making them visible targets of white anger and fear. The irony is even greater when we recognize that the people who have the greatest reason to be angry and fearful are Blacks and other people of color, and yet the growing white nationalist movement in the US claims that whites are discriminated against and should fear Blacks.

The Gulf between Blacks and Whites

Having privilege and not having privilege also leads to differences in how people experience the world, and those different experiences lead white Americans and Black Americans to understand the world around them differently. For example, if white children grow up being taught that police officers are in their communities to protect them, and their experiences growing up are consonant with that belief, then they see the police as a lawful force for good. If, on the other hand, Black children grow up being taught that they need to speak and behave carefully around police officers because they may harm them in some way if they do not, and their experiences and the experiences of others around them are consonant with that belief, then those children will grow to adulthood seeing the police as a force to fear.

In 1995, many whites in the US were stymied by the Black response to the OJ Simpson verdict. Simpson, an African American former football star and major television personality, was accused of murdering his wife, Nicole Brown Simpson, and a man named Ron Goldman. The evidence appeared to be overwhelmingly against Simpson, but the jury, which comprised nine Blacks, one Hispanic, and two whites, returned a not guilty verdict. A CNN-Time Magazine poll found that 88% of Blacks supported the verdict while only 41% of whites believed that the "jury did the right thing."[11] Whites, who believed Simpson to be guilty, were surprised by the response of Blacks. But many Blacks were not necessarily expressing a belief in Simpson's innocence. They were expressing a belief in the unfairness of the criminal justice system and rejoicing in the fact that one Black man beat it.

The difference in how Blacks and whites respond to the criminal justice system points to both the way our personal experiences as members of our races shape our beliefs about the world and why it is so important for white people to talk with Black people. Until we have open and honest conversations about race, we cannot begin to understand our different perceptions of the world. Earlier in this chapter, we described an interaction in a race dialogue in which a white nurse told a Black man that he was wrong to believe that he and his family had been ignored in the emergency room because they were Black. The man told the nurse that she had no right to deny his experience. The nurse made her comment with the best of intentions. She frequents emergency rooms. She has seen white people ignored. But she has not experienced a world in which virtually every situation leads a Black person to conclude that race is the cause of whatever happens—*because it is the reason that many things happen*. To deny that experience, as the white nurse did, even with the best of intentions, is to exert one's white privilege: "I know your experience because it is the same as my experience."

Bridging the Gulf

How do we begin to address the ways in which we normalize and privilege whiteness so that we can talk more productively about race, especially across racial differences? The first thing that whites need to do is acknowledge that we, in fact, do normalize and privilege whiteness.

The normalization of whiteness is already being questioned in our daily cultural discourse. Fashion designers feature models of color in their runway shows; Black models and actors are appearing on the covers of fashion magazines such as *Vogue* and *Bazaar*; cosmetics companies are marketing makeup lines for a broader range of skin tones and are featuring Black women as the "face" of those makeup lines. The fashion industry has begun an extended conversation about who defines beauty and who represents it.

Hollywood is also talking about the normalizing of whiteness. The absence of Oscar nominations for Black actors, directors, and producers in both 2015 and 2016 led to a Twitter storm with the hashtag #OscarsSoWhite. That conversation resulted in more films featuring Black actors and more Black filmmakers being nominated in 2017, with a Black-themed film, *Moonlight*, winning best picture and two Black actors, Viola Davis and Mahershala Ali, taking home the honors for best supporting actress and actor. In 2018, however, despite the continuation of the conversation, the top Oscar winners were white. The one nominated best film that focused on race, *Three Billboards Outside Ebbing, Missouri*, won awards for two white actors. The following year set the record for most wins by Black nominees, but that success was followed in 2020 with a three-year low for the number of Black nominees. Some people argue that the success of the South Korean film *Parasite*, which swept most of the major awards, marked a return to the success of actors and filmmakers of color. But *Parasite* is not an American film: its director and actors are South Korean. Hollywood's retreat suggests how difficult it is to move beyond using whiteness as the standard. Jon Chu, who directed the 2018 hit, *Crazy Rich Asians*, insisted on using an entirely Asian cast. The spate of news stories about the casting of the film points to how unusual it is to cast an entire film with people of color and how difficult it is to get financial backing for such a film. Why? Because there is a belief, recognized or beneath the surface, that audiences—primarily white audiences—want to see white people on the screen.

We've begun to talk about the fact that we normalize whiteness, at least in some cultural milieus, but we haven't yet shifted toward normalizing difference. It's still noteworthy when we see Blacks and other people of color in situations where we expect to see whites. Someone recently called the Smith College campus police during the summer to report a "suspicious" person who was sitting in a common area but didn't seem to belong there. The police officer who went to investigate discovered a young Black woman, Oumon Kanoute, eating her lunch. The police officer asked her who she was, and Kanoute explained that she was a Smith student who had a summer job on campus. The story created outrage in the community and nationally, with commentators calling it another case of "profiling by proxy." That it happened, however, is not surprising. For many people, it's still not "normal" (meaning that it's not expected) to see a Black person in spaces that have been historically white and in a time frame that is unexpected by the observer. The incident occurred during the summer, not during the academic year when at least some Black students would be seen on a regular basis. And the wide range of areas in which we normalize whiteness makes it difficult for whites to recognize when it exists. We don't question the color of bandages, the absence of Black faces on greeting cards, the absence or scarcity of products on the drugstore shelves for Black hair or skin, the Christmas tree ornaments that feature only a white Santa Claus or white angel. Most whites do not give these things a thought because they accept them as normal. Jeff Jacoby, a white *Boston Globe* op-ed columnist, wrote that the Smith College incident wasn't racist because there were no racial references involved. He concluded that "a minor misunderstanding by a cautious employee was quickly resolved and never escalated into anything dangerous."[12] Callie Crossley, a Black journalist and commentator in Boston, responded that she doesn't want to hear whites "tell me what isn't racist when I live it every day. Nearly every minute of every day."[13] Whites don't see much of the racism around us because we have normalized the behaviors. If Oumon Kanoute had been white, would her presence during the summer on the Smith College campus have seemed suspicious? It's doubtful. She would have simply blended in with "normal" summer life on campus.

If addressing the normalizing of whiteness is hard, addressing the privileging of whiteness is even harder. The very mention of "white privilege" tends to shut down discussions of race. Whites in the conversation often try to shift the discussion to other forms of oppression: "I'm gay or lesbian," "I grew up poor," "I'm Jewish or Muslim," "I'm a woman." Sometimes the comments are intended to show solidarity with Blacks and other people of color. But by equating their oppression with the daily lives of people of color, whites who shift to their experiences as members of marginalized groups deny the experiences of Blacks. Our point is not to measure degrees of oppression or deny the very real negative consequences that many whites have experienced because they are gay, lesbian, poor, Jewish, Muslim, women, or any other marginalized identity. Our point is to acknowledge the particularities of being a person of color and the ways in which white skin protects white people regardless of their identity or identities within marginalized groups.

We often asked our students or participants in workshops to hold onto moments of discrimination that they believed they had experienced to help them develop empathy for people of color. We emphasized, however, that for the most part these moments of discrimination were either unusual (for example, a man in a workshop said he couldn't rent an apartment in St. Louis during World War II because he asked his potential landlord, who was Jewish, where the nearest Catholic Church was) or happened only sometimes (for example, the recounting of gays or lesbians who feared coming out when people asked about their romantic partners).

Living in a Black skin is a markedly different daily experience. Black parents have shared stories with us of Black children who try scrubbing their skin to "clean off" the dirt or make it lighter. Some of our white students told us about high school "ghetto parties" where white teenagers would dress up in "costumes" to look like Black teenagers. The students' motives were not all intended to be demeaning. Some of them described Black teenagers as more "colorful," "interesting," and "courageous." What the students failed to understand, however, is that, at the end of the party, they could go home and take off their costumes. They didn't have to continue to live as a Black teen and experience the consequences of black skin.

Whites also sometimes respond to discussions of white privilege by saying, "But I (or my parents) earned the good things that we have. We worked hard for them." It's important to remember that having privilege doesn't guarantee success. To say that one has white privilege doesn't negate the hard work it takes to earn a college degree or be professionally successful. Having white privilege just means that we have some cards in the deck stacked in our favor before we even begin to play the game. As Paul Kivel says, "It's not necessarily a privilege to be white, but it certainly has its benefits."[14]

McIntosh, in fact, questions using the term "privilege." She says that privilege is "misleading" because its connotations are "too positive." She says that what she has called "white privilege" is something that "confers dominance" on one group and doesn't work to benefit all of society. She concludes that we need to "distinguish between earned strength and unearned power conferred systematically." McIntosh argues further that not having these conferred advantages may make members of marginalized groups stronger, while having them makes white people weaker. Her hypothesis is interesting given our experience with the exercise we described earlier in which whites and people of color met in separate groups and talked about their strengths and challenges as members of their racial groups. Blacks often identified as a source of pride the resilience they possess because of their ancestors' enslavement and their own ability to survive the systemic racism that lingers to this day. Whites, on the other hand, often talked about wishing they had the courage of Blacks.

For those white people who have begun to see how white privilege stacks the deck in their favor, a discussion of privilege still often shuts down the conversation because they are consumed by guilt. At the end of the Opportunity Walk exercise, we ask the people at the front of the line to turn around and see who is behind them. The people at the front are invariably white and many of them respond emotionally as they turn and see Latinx and Black people behind them. When we begin to process the exercise, these white people are often unable to participate in the discussion because, as they say, they feel too guilty. They believe they have no right to speak.

McIntosh warns against such guilt. Her goal is not to paralyze whites into inaction but to spur us to action. She asks us to distinguish between the advantages that everyone should have (for instance, equity in the justice system) and the disadvantages that should be placed on no one (for instance, the assumption that you are less intelligent).

Although guilt is an understandable response to recognizing our white privilege and its consequences, we need to overcome its dampening effect on moving forward. It's fine to acknowledge feeling guilty, but it's counterproductive if that acknowledgement leaves us embarrassed, speechless, and actionless, and, therefore, nothing changes. Guilt can positively affect our perspective by providing a deeper foundation for getting to the power of white privilege. When we learn something about the impact of white privilege, we must use it as a corrective measure in both words and actions.

Whites need to face up to the ways that we continuously erase our own racial identity while simultaneously declaring its superiority by normalizing and privileging it. There's a wonderful concept in yoga called *satya*—a Sanskrit word for the concept in Indian philosophy that means "truth without distortion." The quest focuses on finding and facing the truth within ourselves. As white people, we need to find satya to move the conversation on race in the US forward.

Moving the Conversation Forward
Things Not to Do

- Don't say "I'm scared to get pulled over too" after a Black man says that he's scared when he gets pulled over by police when he's driving. You might be nervous that you'll get a ticket if you're pulled over by a police officer, but a Black man knows he might be handcuffed, slammed against his car, or even killed. Genuine conversation about race can only start when we recognize the differences in each other's experiences.
- Don't be defensive when the conversation turns to racism, especially when a Black person raises the issue. Whites tend to respond defensively when Blacks talk about racism because they feel that they are being accused of being racist. Most often, Blacks are talking about systemic racism not interpersonal racism. While each of us likes to believe that we are not

racist in our thoughts, speech, or behavior, we are all complicit in the systemic racism that permeates our culture and institutions. The accusation of racism by Blacks directed at whites usually is intended not as a personal attack but rather as an observation about the reality of Black people's everyday lives in the US. If the comment is about something that you said or did, try even harder not to be defensive. Whites are often unaware that what they say or do hurts people of color. And whites often say and do things that replicate structural racism without knowing what they've done. When this is pointed out, it's important to open up the discussion rather than deny what happened. If you understand why your action or comment was racist, own it and apologize. If you don't, ask for an explanation.

Things to Do

- Listen to the voices and stories of others without interrupting, judging, or interpreting from your own perspective. Active listening is always difficult. How we're feeling physically, things happening in the environment around us (a hot room, noises outside the window), words or phrases that trigger an emotional response in us—these all get in the way of our truly listening to others. Because conversations about race are so fraught with emotional issues that are usually personal in nature, openness to hearing what others have to say is challenging. But whites must listen and learn to take in what people of color are saying rather than chiming in with their own opinions and experience. William Evans, a white former Boston Police Commissioner known for his work in communities of color, was quoted in the *Boston Globe* as having referred to the Black Lives Matter movement as an "anti-police dialogue." A white woman, Maureen Milliken, wrote a letter to the editor in response to his comment, saying: "Even this white lady from one of the whitest states in the country

[Maine] knows that Black Lives Matter is a way to promote the idea that Black people aren't less than white people—a positive pro-understanding movement, not an 'anti-police dialogue.' White people, even top cops, have to stop being defensive and start listening."[15]

• Develop empathy. Empathy is the ability to understand and share the feelings of another person. *Psychology Today* defines empathy further, saying that it is "the experience of understanding another person's thoughts, feelings, and condition from their point of view, rather than from your own." Developing empathy requires the ability to listen to others without judgment and without imposing our perspective on theirs. Some would argue that complete empathy with others is impossible. We agree but working toward empathic understanding of others stands as one of the most important cornerstones of racial accord. Without demonstrable empathy, there can be no trust.

• Acknowledge and, when possible, defer to the voices of Black people. One of the privileges of being white in many situations is the ability to speak. Historically Blacks were often legally not allowed to speak. Today, the issue is that Black voices are often drowned out by whites—sometimes because they are outnumbered, sometimes because they are assumed to add no value to the discourse. As whites, we need to learn how to share the conversational space with those who have been left out. Rather than jumping in to speak at every opportunity, allow others to speak first. And when we do speak, acknowledge what we have learned from Blacks by naming them as the source of our knowledge. Ayanna Pressley, the first Black woman elected to the US Congress from Massachusetts, modeled that behavior during her final act as chair of the Boston City Council. Pressley was presiding over a "listening session," a practice she brought to the Council, in which people directly affected by an issue being considered are allowed to speak uninterrupted about their experiences. Pressley said that she came up with the idea of holding such sessions when she was newly elected. She called Tina Cherry, a Black woman who founded the Louis D. Brown Peace Institute after her son, Louis, was killed by a stray bullet in 1993. She asked her what she could do to help the community. Cherry said "listen." Rather than claim the credit for creating the practice, Pressley acknowledged the person who inspired her to create it, and by doing so, she shared her privilege as an elected official.

Chapter 4

Raising Your Racial IQ

What Whites Don't Know about Living in a Racialized World

"A LITTLE LEARNING IS A DANGEROUS THING." This saying reminds us that we need to be cautious about overstating what we know. Nowhere is this caution more relevant than in race relations. Too often, we believe that we know something, which makes us feel free to express ourselves, only to find out that we were wrong—or worse, never to find out that we were wrong because no one corrects or informs us. The other side of "a little learning" is no learning at all. No need-to-know. Never been told. Never asked. Perhaps because we think we know enough. Perhaps because we haven't encountered what people of color know but whites don't.

One reason that white people cannot and do not talk about race is that we do not know enough to talk sensitively and intelligently or sometimes to talk at all. Why is this? Simply put, we do not know enough because our world unfolds to us in ways that do not spotlight racial experience, even if the focus is on racial topics or incidents. We highlighted this in chapter 3. The news we read and hear, the education we receive, the people we talk with, the subjects that dominate our discourse—rarely do any of these focus on the perspective of how people of color live their lives, and how it came to be that way. Another factor is that we do not consciously make it our responsibility to know and to probe the truths and information that lie deeply in our country's racial history and current racial discord.

The purposes of this chapter are to reveal what's hidden to whites about the experiences of living day to day as a person of color in the

US, laying bare the consequences of a society steeped in racism; and to offer prompts for strengthening and moving our knowledge into conversations with both other white people and people of color. Our goal is not to chastise whites for what we don't know but rather to establish benchmarks against which we, as white people, can continuously test and push ourselves to know more about the relationship between structural racism and day-to-day experience, thus reducing the "danger" of our ignorance when we talk with others. It is impossible for us to lay out the exact knowledge we need because it is too expansive and, in many areas, quickly outdated. Rather, what we stress is the importance of developing a habit of mind to think differently about race, to work on filling the gaps in our knowledge, and to become less defensive and more comfortable with being corrected so that we can talk more productively with others.

We highlight five areas of white ignorance that come up repeatedly in conflicts and misunderstandings about race. For each, we point to some key information often missed by white people, and we offer suggestions for conversations both with other whites and with people of color. Black Americans often say they are tired of teaching white people about their experience—tired of repeating the same things over and over and tired of the expectation that they will do the teaching. We as whites can and should do more of the heavy lifting to build knowledge and understanding.

The five topics we consider here are ones that many white people may have heard about but usually not beyond general points:

- the historical legacy of racism that is carried into the present day
- the ways the educational system continues to be prejudicial against Blacks and other people of color
- racial disparities in illness and health care
- racial disparities in policing and the criminal justice system
- income inequality and wealth gaps that correspond to race

We invite readers to ask themselves three questions before reading each section:

- What do I know about this topic?
- Where did I learn what I know?
- Have I ever sought more information about the topic and how did I do it?

A personal example demonstrates how the questions might progress. The topic is the care of Black hair. We have two African American sons. We knew that taking care of our sons' hair would be challenging for us as white people. Here are our answers to the questions.

- We knew about daily hair care routines—the importance of combing, brushing, and conditioning.
- A Black woman friend told us that it was critical that we "keep their hair"—meaning that we needed to know how to manage their hair and not have fingers pointed at us, *especially by Blacks*, for lack of hair care. Then, at an adoption conference, we learned how to comb and moisturize their hair from a Black woman who ran a hair salon.
- We sought more information online. We read about how the texture of their hair would change after their first haircut and what hair clipper to buy so that we could cut their hair ourselves. When they were old enough to need a barber, a Black male neighbor recommended a local Black barber. The barber taught us more.

There remained a lot that we didn't know about Black hair. We recognize now that we had many misconceptions caused by both our lack of experience and need-to-know prior to adopting our sons.

African Americans in Historical Context

In this section, we focus on African American history. Our intention is not to neglect the history of Indigenous people, people of Asian descent, or Latinx people. Their histories are critically important to any larger discussion of race in the US and are further complicated by the contentious national discussion about immigrants and immigration. We also do not intend to gloss over tensions both within racial groups and between racial groups other than Blacks and whites. For our purposes, however, we focus on Black history and experience, and white lack of knowledge about both. Before you read this section, remember to answer the three questions we suggested earlier as they relate to African American history.

The history of Blacks in the US is complex and includes both trauma and celebration. Most Americans know that Blacks were enslaved and brought here from Africa. In primary school, we are taught that Abraham Lincoln freed the slaves with the Emancipation Proclamation in 1863. For many, Black history then ends until the early 1950s and the advent of the civil rights movement. Some baby boomers remember Rosa Parks' refusal to give up her seat on a bus to a white man in 1955, the 1963 March on Washington, the Voting Rights Act of 1965, riots in Black areas of major urban centers in the late 1960s, and Martin Luther King's assassination in 1968. Younger people may have learned about some of these events in school. Today most Americans are aware of numerous high-profile cases of police killing young Black men and the rise of the Black Lives Matter movement. And every February during Black History Month, we are reminded of important people and events in Black history. But generally, we know little else beyond a few headlines and popular culture depictions of Black historical events or famous African Americans (for example, the films *12 Years a Slave, Hidden Figures,* or *BlacKkKlansman*). Our purpose is not to cover all African American history or even a small part of it but to demonstrate how little white Americans know about the history of Blacks, and to show how that history shapes present-day beliefs, attitudes, and experiences of Black people.

In August 1619, a ship holding 20 to 30 enslaved Africans anchored at Port Comfort in the British colony of Virginia.[1] Over the next 250 years, 12.5 million Africans were kidnapped and brought in chains across the Atlantic. Nearly 2 million didn't survive the journey, which came to be called the Middle Passage. Slavery became the foundation of economic life of the British colonies in America, especially in the South, where cotton fueled economic growth. Grown and picked by the enslaved, cotton was the country's most valuable export. Although slavery had been legal in all thirteen of the original colonies, between 1774 and 1804, the northern states outlawed it and shifted to paid labor. Slavery, however, was instrumental in building the northern economy. The textile mills of the North relied on cotton grown in the South.

As we said in chapter 2, race is not a biological truism but a social construct relied on by our country's founders to justify enslavement. When enslavement ended, race continued to serve as an artificial construct that justified segregation and continued brutality against Blacks.

With the Emancipation Proclamation in 1863, President Lincoln freed the slaves in the Confederate states. The four border states that had not seceded from the Union—Missouri, Delaware, Maryland, and Kentucky—were not included. The passage of the 13th Amendment to the Constitution in 1865 formally ended the institution of slavery. Although the 13th Amendment was signed on February 1, 1865, Texas did not free the enslaved until June 19, which was designated Juneteenth Independence Day or Freedom Day for African Americans. Even then, Texas legislators urged freed slaves to stay with their former enslavers. Some enslavers waited until after that year's harvest to tell their slaves, while others shot or beat those who tried to leave.[2] Although Juneteenth Independence Day (known as Juneteenth among Blacks) is a recognized holiday in all but four states, it is not a federal holiday. Many whites have now heard of it because news media covered the controversy that arose when President Trump scheduled a campaign rally in Tulsa, Oklahoma on that date. Most, however, don't know what it commemorates. Freed slaves, who continued living primarily in the South, often could not celebrate the holiday because segregation laws that spread across the

South following the end of the Civil War prohibited Blacks from using public places or parks. Life in the postwar South gave African Americans little to celebrate.

Conversation Prompt: Use this prompt with a conversation group in which at least two people are Black. Discuss what should be done with monuments that celebrate Confederate victories or honor Confederate heroes.

When the Civil War ended in 1865, Blacks in the South enjoyed a few brief years of relative freedom and civil rights during Reconstruction (1865–1877). In 1876, however, Congress agreed to remove the federal troops that had been placed in the South after the Civil War. Southern legislatures, no longer controlled by Northerners, passed laws requiring the separation of Blacks and whites in public transportation and schools, and later extended to parks, cemeteries, theaters, and restaurants. The years in which segregation was legally sanctioned in the South became known as the Jim Crow era, named for a minstrel routine that was a derogatory term for Blacks.[3]

In 1896, the Supreme Court ruled 7 to 1 in *Plessy v. Ferguson* that Louisiana's Separate Car Act was constitutional. It required all trains in Louisiana to have separate but equal accommodations for Black and white passengers and prohibited each from entering the cars of the other. The decision sanctioned "separate but supposedly equal public facilities and services for African Americans and whites"[4] and allowed Jim Crow laws to flourish throughout the South. The South remained legally segregated until 1954 when the Supreme Court unanimously ruled in *Brown v. Board of Education* that "separate but equal" classrooms violated the 14th Amendment.

Whites are especially unfamiliar with the horrific violence perpetrated by whites against Blacks throughout the US in the first half of the 20th century. One of the deadliest years was 1919, when Black men, women, and children were burned, beaten, hanged, or shot in at least 60 race riots. The following list highlights only a few.

- April, Jenkins County, GA: 6 people die when whites attack Blacks
- May, Charleston, SC: 3 Blacks die when whites led by US Navy sailors attack Blacks
- July, Longview, TX: 4 people die, Black housing district destroyed when whites attack Blacks
- July, Bisbee, AZ: police attack a Black cavalry unit
- July, Washington, DC: 10 whites and 5 Blacks die in 4 days of mob violence against Blacks
- July, Norfolk, VA: white mob attacks homecoming celebration for Black veterans returning from World War I
- July, Chicago, IL: 25 Blacks and 15 whites die in riots after whites throw rocks, killing a young Black man swimming toward white section of beach
- September, Elaine, AR: over 200 Black men, women, and children killed when whites attack Blacks meeting with union organizers

July 1919 became known as the Red Summer. Sadly, most white Americans know nothing about it. History books ignore it, and most museums don't acknowledge it. Even young Blacks growing up in communities marked by violence during that time period often don't learn about it. For example, after the white-on-Black violence in Elaine, Arkansas, some Blacks were forced to leave the state and had their land stolen. People in Elaine today say that they were not told about the massacre when they were growing up.[5]

The white-on-Black violence of the Red Summer contributed to "generations of black distrust of white authority"[6] and laid the foundation for the continued segregation of towns and cities long after the end of legal segregation. After the Chicago riots, for example, restrictive covenants were used to ensure that Blacks could not buy homes in white neighborhoods. Later, when restrictive covenants were no longer legal, whites would send messages to homeowners' associations telling white owners not to sell their homes to Blacks, ultimately leading to the concentration of Blacks who live on Chicago's South Side.

The legacy of the Red Summer is not, however, just about Black oppression, distrust of whites, and de facto segregation of many cities and towns. It is also about resistance. Blacks weren't just victims. Many fought back. Black newspapers such as the *Chicago Defender* provided "an alternative voice that represented why African Americans deserved to be here, deserved equal rights and were, in some cases, justified in fighting."[7] This resistance, just like the resistance of enslaved Blacks, planted the seeds that underlie so many other events: the civil rights and Black power movements, Tommie Smith and John Carlos raising their black-gloved fists during the Olympic ceremonies in 1968, Colin Kaepernick and other football players taking a knee during the national anthem, the Black Lives Matter movement, and numerous other demonstrations of Black resistance against racial inequity.

We've painted a pretty bleak picture of Black history here, and although it's important to remember and acknowledge this history, it's also important to recognize that Black experience encompasses more than oppression. Blacks celebrate the contributions of Black artists, writers, intellectuals, scientists, musicians, athletes, teachers, and innovators, along with many cultural traditions passed through generations. Amy Sherald, the African American artist who painted the official portrait of Michelle Obama, talked about a pivotal moment in her career when she saw a retrospective of the African American artist Kara Walker's work. As she processed Walker's images in the context of her own experience as a Black girl growing up in the South, she "realized in that moment there was no conversation happening around just black people being black. Culturally we're presented in one way. It's like Africa, slave boat, slave, civil rights, President Obama…. And that's supposed to be the happy ending. But there are so many different tropes of who we are, and how we exist, and all that needs to be expressed as well."[8]

Conversation Prompt: If you are in a book group, have your group read *The Warmth of Other Suns* by Isabel Wilkerson, which tells the story of America's Great Migration from 1915 to 1970, when millions of African Americans from the Southern US moved to the Midwest, Northeast, and West. Talk about the book using the discussion questions Wilkerson includes at the end of the book. If you are not in a book group, convene a small group to read and discuss the book.

Knowing and understanding Black history helps us begin to understand Black life today. In subsequent sections, we look more specifically at particular aspects of contemporary Black life, exploring racial disparities in education, health, criminal justice, and wealth.

Racial Disparities in Education

As you begin reading this section, remember to ask yourself: What do I know? Where did I learn it? Have I sought additional information?

Our educational system sits at the heart of what we know and how we learn to know. It's fair to say that what children learn about race in educational settings is limited to a sketch of major historical moments, prominent figures, and current issues. Students learn more today than in prior generations when the curriculum rarely stretched beyond Booker T. Washington, Frederick Douglas, and Harriet Tubman, eventually including Martin Luther King, Jr. and Rosa Parks. Post-1960s, the civil rights movement made its way into the curriculum, but not everywhere and not without controversy. The experiences of Black children and other children of color lie well beyond these historical figures and moments. Whites know little about those experiences, but they are front and center for people of color. As white people, we need to be better informed.

Brown v. Board of Education

One of the most well-known legal cases in the US is *Brown v. Board of Education*. The Court ruled unanimously that "separate educational

facilities are inherently unequal." The case nullified the legal basis for
segregated schools.

Nearly seventy years later, however, many schools in the US remain segregated as a result of de facto segregation, which occurs
because of "facts"—notably where people live. Racial segregation
created by patterns of residential segregation is the norm today.
Large urban areas are home to the largest number of students of
color, with suburbs and rural areas dominated by whites. New York
schools are the most segregated in the nation,[9] with New York City
and Buffalo topping the list. In Massachusetts, Boston went through
a painful and conflict-ridden experience with school bussing from
1974 to 1988, the goal of which was to desegregate the schools. In
2018, the *Boston Globe* reported that "nearly 60 percent of the city's
schools meet the definition of being intensely segregated—meaning
students of color occupy at least 90 percent of the seats. Two decades
ago, 42 percent of schools were intensely segregated. Many of these
schools are low performing."[10] Think about that statistic. Well over
half of the schools in Boston have at most 10% white students. The
reverse is found in suburban schools. Although the most segregated
schools are in the Northeast, de facto segregation exists throughout
the country:

- The public schools in California are 84% Black and Latinx.
- Half of all Black students in Illinois attend schools in which
  90% or more of the students are minorities.
- 90% of urban public schools in Texas are Black and Latinx.
- In Michigan, Black and Latinx students attend schools that
  are 90% minority.[11]

On average, whites are likely to attend a school where three quarters
of the students are white, while Blacks attend a school where one half
of the students are Black and only one quarter are white.[12] Although
laws cannot be used to segregate students by race, segregated neighborhoods result in an alarming racial separation.

Conversation Prompt: Take a few minutes and jot down the benefits and disadvantages of going to a school where most of the students look like you. Next jot down the benefits and disadvantages of going to a school where few, if any, students look like you. Then jot down the benefits and disadvantages of going to a diverse school where students see others who look like them and those who don't look like them. Discuss your lists with the group.

The Curriculum

Some whites have questioned their own educational experiences based on how diverse their schools were. For example, Marlene's white students from white rural areas often said that they selected a college in Boston because they wanted the experience of going to a diverse school. Few of us, however, have thought about what we learned or didn't learn in school as it relates to race.

First, there are issues of what is taught. All schools struggle with priorities about curriculum. More STEM? More writing? More history? More about the history of race? More literature by non-white authors? If so, what should be removed from the curriculum? Content related to race continues to be very limited, even in school systems committed to breaking through the ignorance barrier.

Take history for example. We assume students learn about slavery. Yet, recent research concluded that high school students know little about it, with less than 10% being able to identify it as a central cause of the Civil War.[13] The same study found major inadequacies in over half of the textbooks that were examined, with striking omissions in showing slavery's links to Reconstruction, the Great Migration north, the civil rights movement, and systemic racism today. The severing of the past from the present belies a more general ahistorical trend that leads to misunderstanding "the racial divide." We are not arguing that Blacks know US history better than whites. But history is interpreted differently. A Pew Research Center poll found that more whites than

Blacks believe that *states' rights* rather than *slavery* was the main cause of the Civil War, with the divide sharpest for younger Americans.[14] Most African Americans learn about enslavement from their families from the time they are young children. White children, on the other hand, rely on school textbooks and curricula to learn about slavery. All too often, what they learn is limited or taught in ways that gloss over the reality of slavery as both the engine that drove America's economic prosperity and the dehumanizing horror it perpetrated on Black people. Slavery, however, has consequences today in the lives of Black Americans.

The Southern Poverty Law Center's Teaching Tolerance program concludes that: "Teaching about slavery is hard. It requires often difficult conversations about race and a deep understanding of American history. Learning about slavery is essential if we are ever to come to grips with the racial differences that continue to divide our nation."[15] If the conversations are difficult in school, they will certainly be difficult in other contexts.

In elementary school, slavery is often viewed as too difficult for young children to handle, leading to either no lessons or very limited introduction of the topic as a terrible thing that happened in the past: end of story. When slavery is covered, teachers are often ill-equipped to help young children deal with the emotional consequences of talking about it. After our son's fifth grade teacher talked about slavery during Black History Month, the mother of one of his friends called to say that her son came home and cried because he was so upset that his friend's ancestors were enslaved and treated badly. When we talked with the teacher, she was surprised that the young boy had reacted that way and that he hadn't said anything in class. Yes, just like adults, children often don't say anything until they are talking in a safe space.

More generally, we need to be alert to what students learn throughout the curriculum, not just in their history lessons. Is race embedded in topics that are not explicitly about race? Are students reading books that include race as more than a problem? Do they read books by authors of color?

Many whites simply have no reason for ongoing vigilance about what is being taught. White parents might be aware in general of what's in the curriculum, but as children advance through school, parents recede as educational overseers. White parents can and should do more to be aware of the specifics of the curriculum about race, and we can and should raise concerns to teachers and other school personnel, rather than leaving this responsibility to parents of color.

Personal Prompt: How might a parent raise concerns to a teacher in a constructive manner about how race is included in the curriculum? What would be the best way to express dissatisfaction or offer a suggestion to an elementary school teacher or a high school teacher?

Conversation Prompt: In a mixed-race conversation with people who have children in school (elementary or high school), share a time you talked with a teacher about a concern you had with your child's performance in class or about what your child was learning. Compare the experiences. Were they similar? Different? How? If different, what do you take away from learning about those differences?

Fast-forward to college and stay on the topic of history. It's true that today's college students tend to value diversity and inclusiveness. The college curriculum, though, still leaves gaps in what students learn about the historical aspects that affect today's racial climate. A study of the top 75 higher education institutions found that only one-third required any type of US history, even for history majors.[16] Further, that statistic gives no information about what is included about race in the courses that are offered or required.

History, of course, is only one topic. What students do learn about race tends to be crammed into diversity requirements or covered in courses on broader topics or within majors other than history, such as English, sociology, and political science.[17] Most higher education accrediting agencies require some treatment of race and diversity, and some institutions mandate that diversity be included throughout the curriculum. That's both good and bad. Good because at least there is some attention to its presence or absence. Bad because it means that, in the 21st century, race is not taken for granted as included in what students learn. Unlike white students, students of color feel this and react to it because they have been noticing when they are included or excluded in all domains of their lives.

Conversation Prompt: For those who have children in college, talk with them about what they are learning about race in their classes and how race is talked about on campus. For those who do not have children or whose children are not college-aged, try to talk with either some teachers you know or friends/relatives who are in college.

Teachers and Professors

Everyone wants good teachers who know their subject and effectively engage students. The racial identity of teachers, however, also bears on learning. Whites need to understand that people of color notice the racial identities of teachers, while most white people do not unless the teacher is not white.

Personal Prompt: Think back to your high school experience. Did you have any teachers who were Black, of Asian background, Latinx? If so, what subjects did they teach? If not, do you recall being aware of the absence of teachers of color? Do you think having teachers of color made a difference? Do you remember school personnel other than teachers who were not white? What work did they do?

In 2016, 51% of children under eighteen years of age in the US were white, 14% Black, 5% Asian, and 4% multiracial; 25% identified as Hispanic.[18] The profile of teachers' race differed considerably: 80% of public school teachers identified as white/non-Hispanic, 7% as Black/non-Hispanic, 9% as Hispanic, and 2% as Asian.[19]

Although the diversity of teachers has increased over the years, it remains difficult to attract and retain a diverse teaching staff, largely because salaries lag behind other professions. The diversity gap means that all children are more likely to be taught by white teachers and to see too few teachers of color as role models. Students of color benefit in many ways when they are taught and mentored by teachers of color, including higher test scores and greater likelihood of graduating from high school and succeeding in college.[20]

The demographics of the teaching profession also mean that parent interactions with teachers are most likely to be with white teachers. White parents may not think much about this, but Black parents and other parents of color definitely do. Any of the factors that bear on interracial interaction come into play when parent-teacher races differ.

Many Black parents say that white teachers often have low expectations for their children. There is good reason for their concern. For example, a major research study using national data examined the degree to which *the same student* was evaluated differently by teachers of a different race. White teachers were 20% less likely than Black teachers to expect the same Black student to earn a college degree.[21]

Student Experiences

Whites have little understanding of what it's like to be a student of color. We're white, so how could we? It's striking to hear students of color comment about being singled out and put on the spot in class asked to respond to some issue as an *African American* or *Chinese American* or *Latinx*. For example, a professor asking a Black student "What do Blacks think about interracial dating?" Students of color told us stories—some of them horrifying—about comments in and out of class that made them uncomfortable. For example, a fellow student asking a Black woman, "Are you on the basketball team?" In addition, racial slurs and names are still uttered in the school environment, and racist graffiti appears frequently on school and campus property.

We also heard stories about not being noticed at all as teachers and other students make statements stereotyping people of color or washing over their differences. One example is the frequent references to Africa as a country rather than a continent, or the attribution of "Asian" to different nationality groups such as Japanese, Chinese, Indian, Vietnamese, and many others. Another example is the statement that Blacks are athletically gifted and Asians have math and science abilities. Along with showing a lot of ignorance, such comments and questions lack empathy.

As white parents of Black children, we knew we had to rely on Black friends and Black parents of Black children to coach us on how to monitor what our children said or didn't say to us about their experiences at school, and to be ready to talk with a teacher, coach, or administrator. We missed a lot. Some of what we missed we learned from our kids when they were older, and it was shocking and personally embarrassing. For example, we hosted a Passover seder when our sons were in college to which they invited several of their high school friends. At one point in the evening, we discussed racial issues, and one of us commented that we were grateful that the boys hadn't experienced a lot of racism in high school. Their friends (two white and one Black) looked at each other and our sons, and one of them finally said, "That's not true." Each of the young people, including our sons, began to share stories with us of things that had happened that our sons never told us about. We're certain there's much more we will never know about.

In her book *A White Teacher Talks about Race*, Julie Landsman recounts that principals often told her that teachers say Black boys are impossible to work with because they are hyperactive and uncontrollable, but they ignore this behavior in white boys who act out.[22] If teachers expect Black boys to be hyperactive and hard to control, then staying on task may be over-rewarded. And if a Black boy does not conform to these stereotypes, then a teacher may be pleased with any level of consistent performance. Similarly, Latinx boys may be over-rewarded for adequate academic performance simply because of the expectation that they are less likely to graduate than white boys.

This pattern also occurs in college. Faculty may have lower expectations for Black and Latinx students and higher expectations for students of Asian ancestries. Or they may boost the grades of Black and Latinx students because they want to be able to say they are not prejudiced. These practices are difficult to document, but we have heard examples numerous times.

Racial consequences also exist in early childhood education. Data show that Black children, who make up about one-fifth of preschool enrollment, received close to half of the suspensions.[23] This racial disparity in preschool is startling.

It's easy for a white person to see racist and racially related incidents or situations in schools as isolated examples rather than part of the structural racism that permeates the educational system. We need to understand what is going on and to talk more constructively across race about the patterns that exist and our perceptions of them.

Conversation Prompt: Do you think that diversity is important in the educational setting? Why or why not? What aspects of diversity are more or less important—curriculum, student body, teachers, staff and administrators?

Race and Health

We live in an age of advances in health care along with concerns about the rising cost of medical treatment. It's dizzying to keep up with breaking news about research that tells us what we should or should not do to stay healthy, and now, in the age of the coronavirus pandemic, news about vaccines. No wonder that health care is front and center in political debate.

After you've probed what you know about health issues for people of color, move to this question for reflection.

Personal Prompt: Reflect on your own health and that of family members and/or those racially and ethnically similar to you.

• What are the major illnesses and causes of death that concern you—because of family history or your own experience?
• What differences, if any, in health and illness are you aware of that align with racial differences?
• Do you and those you care about have adequate insurance?

Each person's health profile is affected by a range of factors—diet, physical activity, ancestry and genetics, race and ethnicity, income, cultural beliefs and practices, access to health care, perceptions of medical personnel, and even one's zip code. Overall, we live longer than our ancestors because of advances in health care driven by research and technology, improvements in sanitation, public health and safety regulations, and education. The average person in 1900 lived to be 47.3 years old. Those born in the US in 2017 have a life expectancy of 78.8 years—a gain of more than 30 years.[24]

Underlying average life expectancy are complexities related to race.[25] The life expectancy for white females surpasses African American/Black females by almost 3 years (81.2 to 78.5), and white males surpass African American/Black males by 4.5 years (76.4 to 71.9). The American Heart Association concludes that these differences are "largely attributable to [African Americans] having a higher rate of heart attacks, sudden cardiac arrest, heart failure, and strokes than white Americans."[26]

Digging deeper into the health profile shows alarming and consistent patterns that underlie health challenges for non-Hispanic Blacks in the US. Consider this sampling of information.

- Non-Hispanic Black mothers experience the highest infant mortality rate at 11.4 per thousand, compared to the national average of 5.96 and 4.9 for white mothers.[27]
- Non-Hispanic Black adults have the highest hypertension rates at 44%, compared to 30.8% for the total population and 29.6% for whites.[28]
- Approximately 47% of the population of Hispanics and non-Hispanic Blacks suffer from obesity, with childhood obesity alarming in both groups.[29]
- For those 65 and older, African Americans followed by Hispanics have the highest rates of diagnosed Alzheimer's disease and dementia, at 13.8% and 12.2% respectively—about 2% higher than non-Hispanic whites.[30]

No single cause underlies these health liabilities. We can, however, get a sense of what's going on by looking at several factors that most whites know little about, including risk factors and problems within the health care system linked to structural racism.

Health Risks

The National Center for Health Statistics reports that higher death rates for Blacks stem from heart disease, cancer, homicide, diabetes, and perinatal conditions, which together account for a loss of over one year in life expectancy.[31]

Why do such disparities exist? It's difficult in some cases to sort out race from where a person lives and their economic situation. Yet, an aggregate of specific issues impacts Black people differently than white people or those of other racial groups.

Most of us are aware of the rise in diabetes and its health consequences because it's covered in the news. Until the coronavirus pandemic, whites were likely less aware of the higher rates of diabetes in the African American population, which are linked to obesity, genetic traits, and insulin resistance. Heart disease, stroke, and hypertension all share common causes: obesity, lack of exercise, stress leading to high blood pressure, diet. For African Americans, researchers have identified adverse economic and social factors, plus cultural patterns related to preference for larger body mass as especially significant in reducing life expectancy.[32]

Stress is also a major factor in the health consequences for Blacks in the US—stress caused by living in a racially charged society. We've emphasized that discrimination continues to abound. The collective tolls of race accumulate with "driving while Black," "shopping while Black," and simply "being Black" in the United States. A Jamaican man recounted his experience when he moved to New Orleans for college and for the first time faced the penalty of "walking while Black."[33] Although his home streets weren't safe and needed to be navigated, race was not the issue. That changed in the US. Within days, he noticed "that many people on the street seemed apprehensive of me: Some gave me a circumspect glance as they approached, and then crossed the street; others, ahead, would glance behind, register my presence, and then speed up; older white women clutched their bags; young white men nervously greeted me, as if exchanging a salutation for their safety." Googling the term "walking while Black" yields many stories and research—more jaywalking citations, fewer cars slowing down at intersections, fines for walking in the roadway where sidewalks are present. It all adds up to more stress. Most white people do not even think about such issues.

One factor related to life expectancy and race that many whites hear about is the homicide rate, but misconceptions abound. Black men and women have higher death rates from homicide than do whites. In 2017, for example, Blacks/African Americans accounted for 52% of all homicide victims—even though Blacks make up only 13% of the population.[34] We sometimes hear that "they [meaning Black people] are killing each other." Black-on-Black homicides do exist, but the rate of white-on-white homicides is similar. The higher number of deaths by homicide for Blacks relates to education, urban conditions, racial profiling, and stress related to living in a racialized society—to name just a few of the major causes.

Medical Care

First, consider the availability of health insurance. Prior to the implementation of the Affordable Care Act (ACA) in 2013, people of color were less likely to be insured than whites.[35] The ACA boosted health care coverage for everyone, especially people of color. But the improvement stalled during the Trump administration, largely because uninsured people of color are *more likely than uninsured whites to live in states that did not accept federal dollars to expand Medicaid.*

There are also issues within the medical care system that uniquely affect Black patients. One is the dearth of Black doctors. In 2018, for example, only 6.2% of medical college graduates identified as Black/African American.[36] The shortage matters because, according to NBC health journalist Dr. Shamard Charles, "black patients are more likely to feel comfortable with black doctors and more likely to adhere to certain preventive measures delivered by black doctors.... And black doctors are more likely to practice in underserved communities."[37] The shortage of male doctors who are Black has been highlighted in the news mainly because of a steady decline of Black male applicants to medical colleges.[38]

Black patients are under-treated for pain management compared to white patients, and white medical students continue to believe that Blacks feel less pain than whites.[39] The belief that Blacks feel less pain can be traced back to slavery when white enslavers justified their brutality by arguing that Blacks didn't feel pain. That such a belief persists today among doctors and medical students may explain why Blacks feel more comfortable with Black doctors.

Conversation Prompt: Discuss your preferences for doctors you might see for various issues—general health and specialists. Do you have age, gender, or race/ethnicity preferences? Why do you have these preferences? Now think about why Black Americans might prefer doctors of the same race. Why do you think this preference would exist?

Race and the Justice System

As you begin this section, remember to ask yourself what you know, where you learned it, and if you've ever sought more information.

We heard a lot during the 2020 presidential campaign about the need for criminal justice reform, most prominently because the system disproportionately punishes Black and brown people. Among the topics, none has been more emblazoned in reports of race and justice than the ongoing deaths of Black men and women in police confrontations. Blacks are 2.8 times more likely to die in a confrontation with police than whites.[40] It's fair to say that many white people, although outraged by these deaths, feel numb when more news breaks. People of color likely feel each death much more viscerally—no numbness because it's personal, because they know that the victim could have been their child, their parent, or themselves. Racial bias runs throughout the criminal justice system, not just in policing but also in law enforcement more generally, incarceration policies and practices, and the judicial system itself. Most whites need to know much more about the criminal justice system and the mass incarceration of Black and brown people, especially Black and brown men.

Policing and Law Enforcement

Black Americans who have children know when it's time to have "the talk"—that wrenching but realistic conversation about surveillance of Black and brown people by police, state troopers, and security guards in stores and other public places, and also by random (usually white) people for whom a Black presence provokes suspicion. We knew nothing about the mandatory talk until the Black parents of a friend of one of our sons told us that they weren't allowing their older son to get his driver's permit. They explained that they had the talk with him about how to respond when he gets pulled over by a police officer, but they were not confident that he would follow their instructions for what to say and how to behave. When our sons became old enough to drive, we had the talk. And we had other talks about why their white friends could take the train into Boston by themselves at a relatively young age but they could not and about why we hovered nearby when we let them go into a store unaccompanied by us.

Although many white people believe that surveillance of Black people is an outrage, they also believe it's rare. It's not. It's frequent, and few if any Blacks are exempt, regardless of social class, occupation, age, or residence. In 2019, SZA, a well-known Black singer and songwriter, reported that she was accused of stealing while shopping in a Sephora store in Calabasas, an upscale Los Angeles suburb, and the police were called. One time when Marlene was teaching a graduate class on cultural differences, she asked the largely white class if they knew what "DWB" meant. Two white women in the class started giggling and looked at a Black male classmate. Marlene asked what was so funny. One of them said they hadn't known what DWB meant until the previous week when they were riding in a car with their Black male classmate, who was driving, and he was stopped by a police officer for no apparent reason. The officer didn't issue a ticket, just checked his license and registration and asked him some questions. When they drove away, the Black student said to his white classmates, "That was a DWB—driving while Black."

A Stanford University study of nearly 100 million traffic stops from 2011 to 2017 documented "a pattern of racial disparities in traffic stops…which points to pervasive inequality in how police decide to stop and search white and minority drivers," and showed fewer stops of Black drivers at night when the skin color of the driver is less visible.[41]

More broadly, tensions among police departments, prosecutors, and people of color have led to conflicts in many cities. Although white people can grasp racial profiling conceptually, it's not likely they can empathize with what it does to a person of color's level of trust in the police.

Surveillance likely accounts for a sizeable percentage of arrests of people of color, often unjustified, and evokes fear and mistrust. Every white person needs to contemplate what it would be like to be truly fearful every time they see a police officer or security guard. Not carrying that fear with us demonstrates exactly what white privilege is.

Prison

The US is the world leader in the percentage of residents who are incarcerated.[42] The dramatic uptick in the prison population began in the 1980s with the "war on drugs"—now notorious for the heavy sentences given to minor drug offenders. The Sentencing Project reports that "the number of people incarcerated for drug offenses in the US skyrocketed from 40,900 in 1980 to 452,964 in 2017…. The number of people sentenced to prison for property and violent crimes has also increased even during periods when crime rates have declined."[43] Prison sentences have also grown longer, as have the number of prisoners on death row—where the percentage of Black and white prisoners in 2019 was about equal, emphasizing the disproportionate number of Blacks who are sentenced to death.[44]

The Black-white divide is a main theme in the incarceration story. One in 3 Black men born in 2001 will be imprisoned, compared to 1 in 17 white men. For Black women, the divide is even starker: 1 in 18 Black women will be incarcerated, compared to 1 in 111 white women.[45] Blacks make up a vastly disproportionate number of incarcerated individuals. As of April 2020, 37.6% of all federal prisoners were Black, even though Blacks make up only 13% of the population.[46] State prison data in 2017 showed great variability in the incarceration rates for Blacks compared to whites.[47] New Jersey ranks the highest, with 12.2 Black prisoners for every white prisoner. Wisconsin, Minnesota, and Vermont are not far behind, even though the Black population in these states is relatively low.

The lopsided number of Black prisoners results primarily from socioeconomic differences and sentencing disparities. A recent study concluded that "mass incarceration in the United States is primarily a system of locking up lower class men—one which ends up disproportionately imprisoning Black men, since they are far more likely to be lower class than white men."[48] Under the terms of the Anti-Drug Abuse Act of 1986, distribution of 5 grams of crack cocaine carried a minimum five-year federal prison sentence, while it took distribution of 500 grams of powder cocaine to earn the same sentence. Blacks were far more likely to be convicted of distributing crack and whites were more likely to be convicted of distributing powder because crack was sold in smaller quantities, making it cheaper than powder and therefore more prevalent in urban areas. The Fair Sentencing Act of 2010 reduced the sentencing disparities but is not retroactive.

Conversation Prompt: When the crack cocaine epidemic hit the US in the early 1980s, it was defined as a crime wave. In contrast, the opioid epidemic that began in the late 1990s has been defined as the worst public health crisis in recent history. How can you explain the different responses to these drug crises?

Evidence and DNA

We often hear about wrongful convictions. The stories of injustice are many and complicated. The Innocence Project is well-known for successfully using DNA evidence to secure victories for those wrongfully convicted. As of 2019, 367 convictions had been overturned based on DNA data, with 70% of these African American or Latinx men. More broadly, many individuals and groups have worked to overturn a range of cases that were based on faulty evidence, with many involving Black and Latinx men.

The case of the Central Park Five shows how the confluence of racial profiling, interrogation techniques, prosecution strategy, and flaws in evidence can come together to create a wrongful guilty verdict. The case involved a white female jogger who was brutally attacked and raped in Central Park on April 19, 1989. The police apprehended a group of Black and Latinx teenage males who were in the park that night, engaged in what was termed "wilding." Six of them were tried for their role in the attack and rape. One of the six pled guilty to lesser charges and was not part of the ongoing case. There were no DNA matches to link any of the five boys, who were aged fourteen to sixteen, to the attack, and there were many gaps in the narrative that was built to explain what happened. The intense interrogation strategy ultimately yielded confessions—which were later rescinded. All five teens were sentenced to between five and fifteen years, all appealed, but the sentences were upheld. The sixteen-year-old, who was tried as an adult, served thirteen years in an adult prison. Then in 2002, a serial rapist and murderer in prison confessed to the crime. The five men were freed and then sued the city of New York for "malicious prosecution, racial discrimination, and emotional distress." A settlement wasn't reached until 2014, when they were awarded $41 million from the City and $3.9 million from the State.

The Central Park 5 case was featured in a 2012 Ken Burns documentary and a 2019 miniseries created, co-written, and directed by Ava DuVernay, titled *When They See Us* (Netflix). Netflix also released *Oprah Winfrey Presents: When They See Us Now*, which features interviews with the exonerated men. The videos spotlight the horrible implications of racial bias in the justice system.

The Central Park Five case gained national attention, but there are many more cases that we do not learn about.

Conversation Prompt: Choose a group of 5 to 7 people who will commit to watching *When They See Us*—similar to how a book group works. Discuss these points:

• What was most surprising about how the case unfolded?
• Why did the police interrogation proceed in the way it did?
• What was the motivation of the prosecutor?
• Could a case like this happen today? Why or why not?

Wrongful convictions are estimated to be between 46,000 and 230,000.[49] The National Registry of Exonerations reported that, as of October 2016, African Americans accounted for a staggering 47% of the 1900 exonerations in the US—over 125% greater than their representation in the prison population and nearly four times greater than their representation in the general population.[50] Blacks in the US have good reasons to mistrust the criminal justice system and to insist that whites remember that "Black Lives Matter."

The Wealth Gap

We introduced the wealth gap in chapters 2 and 3. Today, Blacks have only 10% of white wealth, a legacy of slavery, Jim Crow laws, restrictive housing covenants, bank redlining, discriminatory application of GI Bill benefits post-World War II, along with continuing employment discrimination. Apart from not knowing the history of wealth inequality in the US, many whites are unaware of how past and present institutional practices maintain, and even widen, the wealth gap.

Institutional/Structural Racism and Wealth

Take redlining for example. In the 1930s, government surveyors graded neighborhoods in 239 cities, identifying them on maps by color: the best neighborhoods outlined in green, still desirable neighborhoods in blue, declining neighborhoods in yellow, and those deemed hazardous in red. Red neighborhoods were discounted as credit risks by lenders, who then charged higher interest rates on mortgages for properties in those areas, a practice that became known as redlining. In the 1930s, these neighborhoods were predominantly African American but also included Catholics, Jews, and immigrants from Asia and southern Europe, all groups who were considered "non-white" at that time. Except for African Americans and Asian immigrants, these groups were accepted into mainstream society over time, identified as "white," and eventually able to buy homes in better neighborhoods at more competitive rates. African Americans by and large remained in redlined areas and unable to buy homes. Today these communities continue to lag behind. Two-thirds of neighborhoods outlined in red in the 1930s are inhabited today mostly by Black and Latinx residents. Conversely, 91% of areas initially outlined in green (the best neighborhoods) remain middle-to-upper income today, and 85% are predominantly white.[51] It's a common misperception that Black neighborhoods are inferior because of the people who live there rather than racist and predatory institutional practices.

As stated earlier, home ownership provides the ability to grow equity used to finance higher education for children or even yourself. It also carries tax advantages that help grow wealth. Limited access to home ownership, especially in more desirable locations, is only one reason why the wealth gap persists. Because Blacks are unemployed, underemployed, or paid less for the same work, they are also less likely to have access to tax-advantaged forms of saving, for instance, company sponsored 401K plans or health savings accounts, and they have less access to retirement benefits.

Further, economic downturns and personal economic shocks tend to affect Blacks more negatively than whites. For example, the Great Recession of 2007 to 2009 worsened the wealth gap. Before the recession, Blacks had 14% of white wealth; by 2018, only 10%.[52] The coronavirus pandemic is expected to increase the gap further. Blacks are also more likely to experience income shocks such as unexpected medical expenses. Think back to the section above on medical disparities. Blacks are less likely to have medical insurance and are prone to a number of health conditions that require expensive medications. When they experience these unexpected bills, they have less access to savings than whites.

Without accumulated wealth (savings, home equity, or other assets), people cannot pay for unexpected expenses, finance a college education, start a business, or risk changing jobs. This is why it's not sufficient to look only at income differences between whites and Blacks. Increasing salaries alone will not shrink the wealth gap. Systematic racism underlies it, which is why the gap persists regardless of education, marital status, age, or income. Median wealth for Black households *with* a college degree is 70% that of white households *without* a college degree.[53]

Reducing the Wealth Gap

There have been numerous suggestions for ways to decrease the wealth gap: providing financial reparations to African Americans, investing in infrastructure improvements in predominantly African American communities, boosting the minimum wage. The wealth gap was a major issue in the 2020 Democratic presidential primary race. Senator Cory Booker proposed opportunity accounts in which every newborn would receive $1,000 to seed a savings account. The government would add $2,000 each year up to age eighteen, depending on family income. This idea merits consideration but alone will not eliminate the wealth gap.

Conversation Prompt: Equality is a fundamental principle of American life. We believe that all people should be treated equally. But equal treatment doesn't always lead to equitable outcomes. For example, women often complain about having to wait in a long line for a public bathroom while the men's room has no line. The solution, of course, would be to have more stalls in the women's room. Unequal treatment but an equitable outcome. Discuss ways of eliminating racial disparities in education, health, criminal justice, and wealth. Do any of them require unequal treatment?

Reparations represent the most widely discussed approach to eliminating the wealth gap and redressing other racial inequities. Americans, however, are deeply divided on the issue. In early 2020, 74% of Blacks favored reparations and 85% of whites opposed them.[54] The dictionary defines *reparations* as the making of amends for a wrong one has done by paying money or otherwise helping those who have been wronged. Reparations to African Americans have long been discussed and even offered. General Sherman's "40 acres and a mule" provided reparations to those who had been enslaved until President Andrew Johnson returned the land to former enslavers.

In 1989, Representatives John Conyers and Sheila Jackson Lee introduced legislation to establish a commission to study and develop reparations proposals (HR 40). The bill has been reintroduced every year but has never made it to the floor of the House of Representatives for discussion and vote. The bill calls for considering reparations for "the institution of slavery, its subsequent de jure and de facto racial and economic discrimination against African Americans, and the impact of these forces on living African Americans."[55]

Although HR 40 has not led to a national conversation, reparations have been implemented in some localities. In 2015, Chicago passed a reparations ordinance that provides $5.5 million to hundreds of African Americans tortured by police from the 1970s through the 1990s. At the initiative of students in 2019, Georgetown University agreed to raise $400,000 yearly to benefit descendants of 272 enslaved people who were sold to keep the college afloat. The funds will be used to support community projects.[56] That same year, Princeton Theological Seminary created a $27.6 million endowment to fund scholarships for descendants of slavery, enhance awareness of the school's links to slavery, and support underserved local communities. An administrator at the seminary called these endeavors "acts of repentance."[57] Although reparations focus on redressing wrongs and creating racial equity, the most significant aspect of any discussion of reparations may be as an act of repentance. As writer Ta-Nehisi Coates said, "An America that asks what it owes its most vulnerable citizens is improved and humane."[58]

Personal Prompt: Are you familiar with any reparations programs either in the US or other countries? Which ones? If you are not familiar with any, do a quick search and read about some. A few you might explore are reparations paid by the US government to Japanese Americans who were interned during World War II, reparations paid by Germany to Israel to help care for Jewish survivors of the Nazi Holocaust, and reparations paid by the South African government to each family of apartheid victims. After reading about these programs, do you believe that the US should provide some kind of reparations to descendants of enslaved persons? What are the pros and cons?

Implications

The history of Blacks in the US and the resulting disparities in education, health, criminal justice, and wealth between Blacks and whites reveal numerous reasons why Blacks often mistrust whites and are reluctant to talk honestly with them.

The negative impacts of race today tend to be trumped by the argument that social class is the more important difference and that if we would just improve educational access and increase wages, everyone's economic well-being would improve. Coates calls this belief a lie and concludes that "the lie ignores the fact that closing the 'achievement' gap will do nothing to close the 'injury' gap,' in which Black college graduates still suffer higher unemployment rates than white college graduates, and Black job applicants without criminal records enjoy roughly the same chance of getting hired as white applicants with criminal records."[59]

As whites in conversation with Blacks, we must acknowledge the pain and suffering of Blacks throughout US history while also recognizing the diversity of individual Black experiences. It's difficult to talk about race without reducing people to being simply "Black" or "brown" or "white." We all have multiple identities, and even within one of those identities, we experience the world differently from others with the same identity. In conversations, we risk failing to see the individual when we focus only on the group. We also fail to see the individual, however, if we don't look at the group. Each of us is shaped by our membership in different identity groups. Those groups also shape how others perceive us. There is a fine line between recognizing each person as an individual and recognizing the importance of their racial and ethnic identities. There will be times when a Black person or a white person may challenge us for being on one side of the line or the other. We must accept those challenges and learn to respond non-defensively and respectfully, and to trust that our partners in these conversations are open and willing to explore these difficulties without judgement.

Moving the Conversation Forward

Things Not to Do

- When someone, whether Black or white, begins to talk about slavery, lynching, segregation, or other horrors that Blacks suffered at the hands of whites in the past, don't say, "That's history, let's focus on the future." As we said in the previous chapter, when a white person says that they don't see color, they are erasing a Black person's identity and experiences. Asking Blacks to move on from their history does the same thing. We can't move on, either as individuals or as a nation, until we are able to acknowledge our history, both good and bad. True reconciliation requires acknowledging the past and seeking forgiveness. But acknowledging collective white responsibility for the past does not mean allowing individual guilt to either paralyze us into inaction or shut us down because "I'm not responsible."

• If you are having a conversation about the Black Lives Matter movement, don't say, "Police lives matter too." Yes, police lives do matter. But a cursory glance at Black history in the US and the daily experiences that Black men and women have had and continue to have with police and the criminal justice system should make clear that Black lives deserve heightened attention. Singling out Black lives highlights the fact that, both in the past and now, Americans have failed to remember that Black lives do matter—not that they matter more than other lives, but that they matter at all.

• Don't start a conversation on a volatile topic (affirmative action, reparations for slavery) by declaring your opinion on the topic. Instead, approach the topic with an open mind. Begin by saying that you want to understand others' positions and how they came to hold them.

Things to Do

• Be open to and curious about African American history. Take responsibility for educating yourself so that you come into conversations knowing something about the historical underpinnings of Black lives and experiences. Be willing to admit when you don't know about something and ask questions. But ask them respectfully and don't be offended if the answer is "Learn about it yourself." Most Blacks have spent their lives being forced to learn about the history and experiences of whites while knowing that whites don't have the same need to learn about the history and experiences of Blacks.

- Listen to the voices of others as they tell you about their history. History is not just a composite of facts. It tells stories and interprets facts. That means there are different views of history. We all view the world through our own lens, a lens that has been formed by our unique histories and experiences. Even if we lived through the same events, my history is not your history. Listen to others without judgement and let them claim their own history.

- Learn to sit comfortably with different and even conflicting interpretations. The goal of conversation is not to achieve consensus on "truth" but to develop trust and empathy for others. Moving ahead on policy issues that will lead to more equitable outcomes for everyone doesn't require total agreement on those policies. It requires a willingness to listen, to compromise, and to seek outcomes that honor the truthfulness of conflicting opinions. Compromise, however, depends on trust, respect, and empathy.

- Seek out sources of information and opinion that differ from your usual ones. Try to find sources that have been created by and for Blacks and other people of color. When you see or hear a story about something that affects people of color, look for more information. Remember, this is about raising our racial IQ. It takes work, but it's well worth the effort.

Chapter 5

Recognizing Differences

Cultural Misunderstandings and Misinterpretations

I N PREVIOUS CHAPTERS, difficulty in talking about race has been linked to limited experience, misunderstanding, prejudice, fear, and guilt. Beneath many of these difficulties lie deeper issues related to culture. This chapter highlights the importance of understanding cultural practices, or those patterned behaviors that coalesce around common identities and often have enduring value. We chose areas where white people misinterpret and even malign cultural practices associated with African Americans, sometimes in ways that contribute to racial misunderstanding and polarization. We selected these topics based on our experience reading and hearing what white people say about the actions and communication of Black people. As white authors, we can neither speak for any person of color nor assume that what we write reflects the cultural practices of greatest importance. We hope that the sampling presented here highlights the importance of *cultural mindedness*, which is the ability to understand that cultural practices play a major role in what we think, say, and do, and we should judge people through *their* cultural lens, not ours.

We introduced the concept of racially identified cultures in chapter 2. To recap, *culture* is the "patterned ways of thinking, acting, feeling, and interpreting" of particular groups. Linguistics offers a helpful metaphor for how culture works. In linguistics, the term *surface structure* refers to the words and sentences we speak; the sounds of language including pitch, stress, and intonation; and the tonal qualities that help give meaning to what is said. The term *deep structure* refers to the grammar that underlies and generates all the sentences we produce. Deep structure is rarely spoken about except for educational purposes. We don't, for example, announce that "I am now going to utter a sentence that is declarative and includes an introductory adverbial clause" before saying, "While walking across Broadway, she got hit by a car."

Using linguistics as a metaphor for the role of culture in understanding and misunderstanding one another can help us see why we often misinterpret or miss things related to race. The surface structure of culture comprises everything we say and do. The deep structure is the storehouse of learning that generates what we say and do. In mainstream American culture, for example, eye contact with others is generally considered a good thing, but this cultural practice is considered rude in many Asian cultures. As with language, we do not usually announce the rules that underlie our eye contact with others, but we know when we see a violation or deviation from what we consider normal: for example, a parent giving a stern reprimand to a child, saying "Look at me when I'm speaking to you" or a statement questioning the honesty of another person by saying, "He wouldn't look me in the eye."

A personal example shows how cultural differences can disrupt understanding. Marlene grew up in New Jersey as part of a small Jewish family. Her parents' close friends were almost exclusively Jewish. Fern grew up in Minnesota, the daughter of a Swedish father and German mother whose parents were immigrants. Both parents had many siblings, and everyone was Lutheran. We recall our first experiences visiting the home of the other's parents. When Fern attended a Passover seder at Marlene's parents' house, she was overwhelmed by the loud voices, interrupting, and arguing that went on throughout the meal. Halfway across the country, Marlene found Sunday dinner at Fern's parents' home overly polite and strangely quiet—enough so that she said she felt like "a bull in a china shop." What occurred in each situation demonstrated different meanings for something as simple as how we interact at the dinner table. American Jewish culture values argument and lively inquiry. "Minnesota nice" describes Fern's family's behavior. The experiences at the Passover seder and Sunday dinner were not random. They demonstrated cultural values and beliefs deep within the history of each community, with that history coming to the surface through the cultural practice of conversation. Yes, not every Jewish person is argumentative and loud, nor is every Minnesotan soft-spoken and nice. But most Jewish people and most Minnesotans will recognize and resonate with the mealtime behavior we've described.

Consider another example. At the 2018 wedding of Prince Harry and Meghan Markle, the bride—a biracial American—chose to include several elements from African American culture in the ceremony, including a sermon given by the Reverend Michael Curry, the first African American to serve as Presiding Bishop and Primate of the Episcopal Church. The sermon followed conventions of the Black sermonic form, with rising tempo, rhythm, repetitions, and vocal expression, moving from a low-keyed introduction to a more vibrant style. The style definitely departed from what members of the royal family might have expected at a royal wedding. A *Chicago Tribune* columnist described the scene: "At various points, Harry's cousin Zara Tindall's mouth hung open, Princesses Eugenie and Beatrice snickered, Prince William seemed as though he was trying not to laugh, Queen Elizabeth and Prince Phillip were stone-faced and many of the other guests were simply stunned."[1] It was clearly a moment of cultural clash on display as the African American preaching style departed from British Anglican expectations. The royal family members likely did not appreciate the historical significance of the African American sermonic form—significant to Black preachers, Black churchgoers, and Meghan Markle. The wedding also included a gospel choir who sang "Stand by Me," a classic R&B song.

Culture lies beneath everything we say and do. It is the blueprint for cultural practices that rise from it, just as a building rises from its blueprint. What we say and do, what we create, and the ways in which we think and organize our beliefs all arise from our cultural grounding.

Personal Prompt: Describe your cultural identity. Can you give it a name? Think about several ways in which that identity frames and shapes your behavior—what you do and how you do it.

Some readers might have had difficulty naming their cultural identity. Others could give a name or even come up with several cultural identities. When we have done this exercise in classes and workshops, the naming part is most often difficult for those whites who do not strongly identify with an ethnic heritage. Some people simply say they are "American." Others might name their regional identity.

The rest of the chapter covers topics that highlight misinterpretations and misunderstandings whites often have about African American culture arising from language and communication, social networks, and clothing and hair.

Conversation Prompt: With a small group of friends of the same race, share what each person thinks are the most obvious cultural differences between most African Americans and most white people. If it helps the conversation, focus on women and men separately.

Language and Communication

No aspect of African American culture is more misunderstood and maligned than the language and communication patterns common to many Black people in the US.

Most of us can quickly identify differences in the way English is spoken. Regional accents and style of speaking stand out the most. We can identify general southern American English with its -y glide that produces *mah* for the word "my," the nasal Midwestern style, certain New York speech with glides that make "talk" sound like *tawk*, and the Boston r-less/broad "a" sound in *pahk the cah in the Hahvahd Yahd.*

Yet, not everyone from each of those regions uses those features. What we hear is all called "American English" but with great diversity. What is taught in schools is usually termed "standard English" (known as Standard American English or SAE) regardless of region. What *standard* means is that rules for grammar and spelling, and conventions for writing have been standardized through a process imposed on how the language is spoken. In other words, what is standard is an ideal that is prescribed by those who have control over the criteria for what is deemed correct. What is standard changes over time, but the conventions always require a type of language blessing from dictionaries, textbooks, and teachers.

Added to regional differences, speech differs based on social class, race, ethnicity, gender, age, education, and neighborhood. In this chapter, we look at what is variously termed "African American Vernacular English," "Black English," "Ebonics," and "African American English." We use the latter term, abbreviated as AAE.

African American English

Well into the 20ᵗʰ century, the language spoken by many African Americans was considered "sub-standard," "non-standard," and "street slang"—all in need of correction, especially if the speaker was to be properly educated. In the 1960s, linguists and communication scholars began serious study of the distinctive elements of English spoken by many African Americans. They documented the systematic structure of elements in AAE that had been thought to be "ungrammatical" and described regularities in the system of sounds, vocabulary, and the prominent patterns and styles of expression typical of many African Americans. Because of the pressures on African Americans to learn and use SAE in school, this research was critically important because it pointed to the folly of teachers making excessive corrections to what they thought were sloppy and ungrammatical forms. For those who want to delve into AAE and how it came into existence, there are plenty of sources.[2] Yet, even after decades of research by many scholars, linguist John McWhorter notes that "the impression remains that Black

English is simply a collection of street expressions, rather than also a system of grammar and an accent requiring native mastery to control fully."[3] He argues, in fact, that AAE is more, not less complex than SAE by laying out detailed linguistic evidence. The "impression" that McWhorter refers to is an attitude about not just the language but also the people who use that language.

We highlight three categories of AAE: stylistic, linguistic, and naming and name-calling. We start with style. African American culture honors the power of "the word." This core idea places value on language itself in a way that differs from what one finds in most of white America, where excellence in speaking may be admired (even if sometimes mistrusted) as "a gift" possessed by the few.

The oral tradition among African Americans carries forward the oral cultures dating back to the African origins of slavery, where the oral mode and the storyteller prevailed as the source of wisdom and connection. Geneva Smitherman, in her book *Black Talk*, links the usage of "Word!" and "Word up!" to the Black oral tradition in which "Yo word is yo bond": "One's word is the guarantee, the warranty, the *bond* that whatever was promised will actually occur."[4] You might recall this adage from Michelle Obama's 2008 speech at the Democratic Convention, in which she said, "My parents impressed on me the values that you work hard for what you want in life, that your word is your bond and you do what you say and keep your promise, that you treat people with respect." Speaking is valued, and speakers are judged for their verbal abilities. The primacy of the word also underlies the verbal expressiveness and poetics found in much of African American discourse—stylized repetition, verbal games, and language routines that create solidarity. Fern recalls comments by a white colleague after an African American man was interviewed for a faculty position. The colleague thought the man's answers weren't direct and that he told too many stories rather than getting to the point. It was precisely his stories, and the eloquence with which he told them, that made the point, but not to Fern's white colleague.

Although those outside of Black communities often admire the verbal skills and talents of African Americans, many whites find AAE overly emotional and loud. Conversely, many African Americans find the speech of whites bland and lacking verbal skill. The contrast pivots on what Smitherman terms the *tonal semantics* in Black expression—"the use of voice rhythm and vocal inflection to convey meaning" through variations in pitch, stress, intonation, volume, cadence, and rate.[5] The tonality of discourse in AAE creates meaning in a way that is distinctive among the many varieties of American English. This is true of the sermonic style of many Black preachers, the rhetorical style of President Barak Obama, and the verbal stylistics of Black teenagers. Many whites admire the verbal abilities and finesse they hear from some African Americans, but just as often, they dismiss or denigrate Black speakers.

For example, at the 2020 Martin Luther King Memorial Breakfast in Boston, both Governor Charlie Baker (moderate Republican, who is white) and US Representative Ayanna Pressley (newly elected Democrat, who is Black) spoke.[6] Representative Pressley spoke passionately, asserting the importance of Black identity amid the rise of white nationalism and racist legislation: "I'm still an Abolitionist," she said, "because my people are still not free…not only because of the new Jim Crow and mass incarceration, but because we don't have economic justice." After she received a standing ovation, it was the Governor's turn. He joked about having to follow "that rant." The audience didn't receive his characterization well, and social media exploded with comments. The key here is that her speech was impassioned, both verbally and vocally—her style, not his. But instead of describing her style in a positive way, he chose a pejorative term. What makes the incident stand out is that Governor Baker said that he agreed with everything she said. We'll take him at his word that he didn't mean to dismiss her. But his spontaneous use of "rant" to describe "passion" did just that. Baker apologized, but the word "rant" came from somewhere deep in his language storehouse to sound dismissive and judgmental.

Representative Pressley, like many African Americans, switches between AAE and SAE. She often speaks deliberatively and in modulated tones, but she also commands a more impassioned style characterized by tonal semantics. Some whites rarely or never hear African Americans in conversation with one another or presenting impassioned statements. Some of those who do hear AAE expressiveness judge it negatively because it doesn't conform to their expectations—expectations based in cultural practices.

We turn next to linguistic examples of AAE often misunderstood by whites. There are many, but these two make the point that AAE is systematic rather than an imperfect version of SAE.

One of the most documented grammatical forms in AAE is the habitual *be* form, which marks permanence and something that is ongoing. In AAE saying "she here" differs from saying "she *be* here." The first means that she's here *now*, while the second means that she's been here *all the time*, that is, she hasn't left. The habitual *be* is more specific than SAE, which requires additional clarification. But it can also be misunderstood by whites who think it's grammatically "incorrect."

Another example is the pronunciation of the word "ask" as *ax*, expressed as "just *ax* anyone" or "she *axed* me." This feature is so stable that it often carries over into the SAE spoken by some African Americans as the only discernable marker of AAE. This pronunciation has roots in the speech forms used by those from whom enslaved Africans first learned English. The long history of varying pronunciations of "ask" include Chaucer's English, in which the word was written as "ax." To the question of why *ax* is used by some African Americans today, McWhorter says it is "as integral a part of being a black American as are subtle aspects of carriage, demeanor, humor and religious practice. 'Ax' is a gospel chord in the form of a word, a facet of black being—which is precisely why black people can both make fun of and also regularly use 'ax,' even as college graduates."[7] At the same time, because ax is often maligned, its use is frowned upon by many educated African Americans.

McWhorter's comment underscores the important function of AAE in creating Black identity. We, as white people, cannot join in that identity, but we can deepen our understanding of why communicative forms—stylistic and linguistic—forcefully sustain that identity. Knowing more about AAE will also help remind us of implicit biases that perpetuate prejudices—judging the intelligence of African

Americans based on thinking their speech is filled with errors, but also judging Africans Americans who do not use AAE with comments such as "You don't sound Black."

Naming Practices

The last topic in this section takes up two practices related to what a person is called: naming and the *N-word*. First, most whites today are familiar with hearing African American names that differ from white names, both the actual names and the spellings—Aaliyah, Deja, DeShawn, D'Andre, Mo'Nique, Trevon, Shaniqua to name a few. Second, most whites also know at least something about the power of what most Americans, regardless of race, consider the most toxic word in the English language—the N-word, which erases a person's name and carries a violent, vile history.

Naming practices are cultural artifacts that tell us something about a person's identity. Americans tend to like first names that are trendy, but some families pass names along through the generations, and some names recur with high frequency over time.

We've heard whites describe African American names as "interesting," "weird," "strange spelling," and "hard to pronounce." We need a little cultural mindedness to get past this.

During slavery, historical evidence shows a range of naming practices.[8] In general, enslavers gave their slaves Christian names, but enslaved people often used their African names within their quarters and for their children. Enslavers commonly gave Biblical names such as Abraham and Sarah, Puritan names such as Charity and Prudence, and classical or historical names such as Plato, Hercules, and Venus—often with satirical or condescending intent. Enslaved people commonly used day-names to denote the day of the week (Monday, etc.) when the child was born or the child's birth order (for example, Sambo or Samba for second son)—both of which continued African naming practices. Some evidence also shows names resulting from converting an African name into a similarly sounding English name, for example, "Kofi" being changed to "Coffee."

Post-reconstruction through the 20th century, evidence suggests that African Americans and whites named their children similarly, with only 3% of African Americans holding distinctively Black names.[9] During the civil rights era, some African Americans embraced African names, both by changing their own names and by giving African names to babies (for example, the first name of President Barack Obama means "blessed" in Swahili, as does the variant Baraka). Since the 1970s, inventive names, African-sounding names, Islamic names, and novel spellings have increased. The pride in naming practices relates to the importance of not just heritage but also creativity. Writing for *Salon*, David Zax says that the names emerge "from a tradition of linguistic and musical invention much like those that gave us jazz and rap."[10]

Conversation Prompt: With a group of friends or acquaintances, have each person talk about their first and last names. Do they carry any particular meaning? Does either name have an historical background or reflect a family tradition? If anyone in the group is adopted, what significance does their name have?

The N-word

The N-word is the most toxic and controversial word in American English. One or two other words would make most people's short list of threatening, degrading, violent terms, but the N-word always tops the list. It's a word with different meanings for Blacks and whites, and it's a word whose meanings vary tremendously by speaker and the context in which it is used.

We are including the use of the N-word because of its fiery history related to racial ideology and its use as both cultural weapon and resource. White people are often confused by the ways in which the word is viewed and used by African Americans. Based on our reading and discussions filtered through our being white, our goal here is to create a better understanding of the cultural shaping of this word over the years.

White people today encounter the N-word in several different contexts: witnessing incidents either literally or in media where the word is uttered by a white person as an attack on a person of color, seeing or reading stories about racist graffiti in public places, reading the N-word spelled out in fiction and non-fiction, hearing Black people use the word among themselves, and listening to rappers and comedians use the word. Some white people also carry vivid memories of the word being used in their neighborhoods and schools. These memories differ depending on how old they are and where they grew up. There is also a history of racist white people calling whites who support and associate with Blacks "N-lovers."

Both of us grew up hearing the N-word but being admonished by our parents never to use it—"it's mean," "it's not funny," or "I don't want to hear that." But we did hear the word uttered in various places and saw it scrawled on buildings and in schoolbooks.

The origin of the N-word goes back to the Latin *niger*, which refers to the color black. The *Oxford English Dictionary* dates the first derisive use of the word for Black people to 1775.

During the civil rights era, the N-word was a weapon hurled at Blacks along with guns, bombs, hoses, and clubs. But even then, some African Americans claimed the word for use among themselves, often pronounced with an *-ah* instead of *-er* at the end. A half century ago, African American author Clarence Major wrote that the N-word "when used by black people among themselves is a racial word with undertones of warmth and good will."[11] Up to then, most whites would have been unaware of that usage, but things began to change by the 1970s. Some whites heard Black comedian Richard Pryor use the word in his routines, notably in his 1974 album, *That Nigger's Crazy*, and some knew that Pryor repudiated his use of the word following a 1979 trip to Kenya.

By the time Pryor had second thoughts, the N-word was on the rise through rap music, and young people were hearing it everywhere. The rapper Ice Cube "claimed the word was a defiant 'badge of honor.'"[12] Teens and young adults gravitated toward the comedy of Chris Rock, who had a lot to say about the N-word, notably in his 1997 stand-up comedy routine captioned "Niggas v. Black People." Although Rock later stopped using it, the N-word moved through popular culture and into the vocabularies of urban white youth, creating confusion and controversy. How could the most noxious, injurious word also be a badge of honor? African American linguist Geneva Smitherman wrote that the frequent use of the N-word "throughout Black Culture…has created a linguistic dilemma…in the crossover world and in the African American community. Widespread controversy rages about the use… among Blacks…and about whether or not whites can have license to use THE N-WORD."[13]

As the controversy continued, academics said the word aloud when teaching about its usage, and they read literary and historical passages aloud that contained the word. In 2002, Harvard law professor Randall Kennedy, who is African American, used the N-word spelled out as the title for a book.[14] He wrote about its history, presenting the viewpoint that the word is being "renovated" with more complex meanings ranging from insult to endearment. The word, he said, is uttered with ease by Blacks to refer to other Blacks and increasingly by whites to refer to other whites "to subvert its ugliest denotation." Kennedy's book dealt with the complexities of reclaiming a word to detoxify it. But uttering the N-word can be a confusing cultural practice for both whites and Blacks.

Kennedy was writing twenty years ago—before the recent eruption of white supremacy, the escalation of police shootings of Blacks, hate crimes, and racist graffiti. With these events, the toxicity of the N-word intensified. On December 24, 2015, the *New York Times* published a letter by George Yancy, an African American philosophy professor at Emory University, titled "Dear White America." Yancy asked white people to recognize their racism and take responsibility for the hurt it causes. In response, he received a barrage of email messages, letters, and voice mail threatening and maligning him, calling him the N-word and every vile racial slur imaginable. His 2018 book, *Backlash: What Happens When We Talk Honestly about Racism in America,* presents the details of the racialized terror unleashed on him, followed by an analysis of what it revealed about racism and white supremacy. You cannot avoid direct confrontation with the N-word when you read his book.

Around this same time, white teachers began to give "trigger warnings" (a metaphor for a range of cautionary statements about content that might be upsetting) to their students before using the N-word in relevant class discussions. News stories began to break about white teachers and staff being disciplined for using the N-word in class, even if trigger warnings had been given. In 2018, controversy erupted at Augsburg University in Minnesota after a student read aloud a passage from James Baldwin's *The Fire Next Time* with the N-word in it, and the white professor followed by using the word during discussion. The professor tried to clarify what happened but was eventually placed on suspension.[15] Kennedy published a scathing critique of the professor's suspension in the *Chronicle of Higher Education*. He argued that use of the N-word during "a perfectly responsible classroom discussion of James Baldwin's rhetoric" should not be policed and doing so was an indictment of both the university and its students. In 2019, in Cambridge, Massachusetts, both students and their Black teacher objected when a white member of the school board in a discussion with students said the N-word when she was explaining what words the internet search filters for students disallow. Reportedly, the Black teacher also used the full word during the discussion. In an op-ed for the *Boston Globe*, Kennedy again objected to the racial double standard for who can utter certain words, calling it a regime that is "wrongly repressive and invidiously discriminatory." A white history professor at the University of Oklahoma was the center of controversy in early 2020 after he gave a trigger warning and then read from a historical document that repeatedly used the N-word. After students complained, the university president instituted racial sensitivity training for all faculty and staff, and wrote a letter to the campus community saying, "It is common sense to avoid uttering the most offensive word in the English language, especially in an environment where the speaker holds the power."[16] These examples reveal the complexities arising from *who* uses the N-word in *what context* for *what purpose*.

The N-word is not likely to disappear. When it's written as graffiti, it needs to be expunged because its use in that context is verbal aggression. But that does not mean the N-word should be censored in writing where it has historical importance or a literary purpose. Some will agree with Professor Kennedy's concerns about banning the full articulation of the N-word for educational purposes. Others will disagree. In more casual usage, though, white people should consider the advice of Black author and public intellectual Ta-Nehisi Coates. Coates told Illinois high school students that "just because certain communities may choose to use a derogatory word ironically among themselves, that doesn't give other people outside that community license to do so." He concluded, "If you're white, just don't use the N-word, period."[17]

Social Networks in African American Culture

With few exceptions, we conduct our lives embedded in social networks, such as family, friendship, religion, activities (sports, hobbies), age, politics, and health issues. Some social networks endure, others are temporary. Some are sustained through face-to-face contacts, others through mediated connections. Think about your own social networks.

Personal Prompt: What social networks in your life are most important to you right now? Name them and the people in them. Are these networks long-term or recent in your life? What benefit do you gain from these networks? Next, identify any social networks once important to you but in which you no longer participate. What changed?

Social networks play an especially important role for groups that have been discriminated against or marginalized. They provide encouragement, offer safety, and help develop resiliency.

White people may know some of the social networks that are important to non-white groups in the US, but they rarely know their history, value, or function. Some Chinese Americans, for example, coalesce around organized activities that include Chinese language instruction for children and social activities for families. Mainland US cities with sizeable Hawai'ian populations often have groups that get together to enjoy food and music.

Social networks have been important for African Americans since enslavement when they functioned for survival and cohesion. We highlight four important network types and show how cultural practices today carry forward long-established traditions: religious and church-affiliated, political, family, and social affinity. Whites may know a little about these networks, but we often incorrectly compare their significance with our own networks (for example, a church group) or do not appreciate their historical significance (for example, fraternities and sororities).

Religious and Church-Affiliated Networks

From the time of slavery, religion played an important role in the African diaspora. As the slave trade began, some of the enslaved were Muslim and some Christian, but most adhered to traditional African rites, rituals, and beliefs. Many who converted to Christianity, often forcibly, surreptitiously organized their own gatherings at night that maintained African traditions. Enslaved preachers were taught to stress obedience to the master when whites were present at Sunday services, but in the absence of whites, "they reformulated their teachings, emphasizing themes of suffering and redemption."[18] Conversion to Protestant Christianity was especially prevalent during the Second Great Awakening in the early to mid-1800s. During this period, itinerant ministers preached that conversion was the path to salvation. The preaching style was emotional and designed to stir animated expressions of faith and the presence of God, and exists today in the "call and response" that occurs between preacher and congregants in traditional Black churches and in some secular settings where Black speakers energize the participation of Black audiences.

Although enslavers saw Christianity as a form of control, many also knew its power in fueling rebellion, as in the famous uprising led by Nat

Turner in 1831. Turner was devoutly religious, and many saw his leadership as a calling from God. Less well-known is Denmark Vesey, who bought his freedom and preached to the enslaved that their salvation, like that of the Israelites, was tied to freedom. He was hanged in 1822 for allegedly organizing a massive revolt from his base in Charleston.

In the North, the Black church movement flourished, with both the Methodist and Baptist denominations allowing ordination of Black ministers. The northern churches became centers for Black association, often assisting enslaved Blacks escaping from the South. After the Civil War, these churches "offered African Americans refuge from oppression and focused on the spiritual, secular, and political concerns of the black community."[19] Over time, many Black churches formed separate denominations that flourish today: African Methodist Episcopal (AME) in 1816; African Methodist Episcopal Zion (AMEZ) in 1821; Christian [initially Colored] Methodist Episcopal in 1870; National Baptist Convention in 1895; Church of God in Christ in 1907; National Baptist Convention of America in 1915; and Progressive National Baptist Convention in 1961. Many congregations of all or mostly Black members also came into existence within the Catholic and Presbyterian denominations.

With its history as a place of refuge and nexus for religious life and secular concerns, Black churches became a central social network that continues in the lives of many African Americans today. Although religious affiliation and church attendance have declined in the US over the last decade, a 2018–2019 Pew Center survey found that non-Hispanic Blacks report the highest religious participation: 78% of Blacks have a religious affiliation, compared to 71% of whites, and 58% of Blacks attend services regularly, compared to 42% of whites.[20] The vast majority of affiliated Blacks are Christian, with most of them Protestant.

Political Networks

Because Black churches span religious and secular concerns, they often function as a political center. Candidates for political office often speak at Black churches. We saw this in the 2020 Democratic presidential primary race, with white candidates and candidates of color headed to Black churches to make their case. Elizabeth Warren, for example, said at a CNN Town Hall that she had asked her pastor how she could better reach African Americans. His answer? Go to the churches.

Most white churchgoers are not used to sermons and speeches by political figures in places of worship, and they often judge such events as oddly out of place. For many Blacks, however, these events are in exactly the right place given the historical importance of the church in all aspects of their lives.

African Americans also organize together in networks related to public office. Because they have been underrepresented in elected positions, there is extra motivation to band together to effect change and develop relationships. The Congressional Black Caucus, for example, was established in 1971 with 13 members—a mere 3% of the total 435 House members. President Richard Nixon refused to meet with the Caucus, leading to its boycott of the State of the Union address. Membership grew to 55 by 2019. The Caucus website states its commitment "to using the full Constitutional power, statutory authority, and financial resources of the federal government to ensure that African Americans and other marginalized communities in the United States have the opportunity to achieve the American Dream." The Caucus has also established a nonprofit Foundation, whose purpose is "to advance the global black community by *developing leaders, informing policy,* and *educating the public.*" They sponsor internships for high school and college students and administer scholarship and fellowship programs.

Most states have groups that function similarly. With 65 members, the Georgia Legislative Black Caucus is the largest. Its website states their purpose is "developing and supporting legislative policy to advance African Americans, People of Color and other underrepresented groups." Members of the state groups network together in the National Black Caucus of State Legislators to improve their own effectiveness as legislators and to support legislation that improves the welfare of their African American constituents. Through meetings and conferences, these organizations provide opportunities for networking and for shared commitment to the legislative priorities most important to people of color.

Personal Prompt: To help understand the work of the Black political caucuses, find a link to the caucus in your state and go through what is included on the website. Reflect on your state context and assess for yourself why the caucus might be important for its members and their constituents.

Family Networks

Many of us know the family reunion as a recurring tradition of importance, an occasional get-together, or an image based on the stories of others. Marlene's Jewish family had no family reunions because there was no family to reunite. Fern experienced a few reunions, which were basically big picnics with 50 to 100 people, sometimes with relatives from out of town, and sometimes occasioned by a funeral. These weren't regular events, and they focused on seeing the relatives and catching up. We have friends who attend more elaborate reunions from time to time, especially friends from the South.

Unlike Fern's family reunions and the reunions many of our white friends have told us about, the family reunions of many African Americans carry significant historical meaning and serve as an affinity network. Slavery broke up families first in Africa and then on the auction blocks where slaves were bought and sold with disregard for the bonds of parent and child, husband and wife, and siblings. As family generations developed, staying together, documenting family history, and honoring ancestry became a critical cultural resource. Family reunions originated as far back as emancipation, when formerly enslaved people sought to locate both blood kin and non-blood kin who were treated like relatives.[21] After the migration of Blacks to the North, reunions became an important network for sustaining relations among those who migrated and those who stayed in the South.

Many family reunions have evolved into major events that extend over a number of days with activities such as barbecues, formal dinners, sports, workshops, contests, awards, family history construction, readings, and musical presentations. One blogger described the essence of this cultural practice: "Black families have reunions to get together, preserve family culture and traditions, share information, and celebrate each and every member that makes up the family. We don't get together every year simply to party, eat potato salad, play Bid Whist...and share laughs. It's much deeper than that for us."[22] The work of Dr. Ione Vargus, founder of the Family Reunion Institute at Temple University, spotlights the importance of these reunions in both reunifying and maintaining the African American family.

We recall hearing our sons' Black barber enthusiastically talking about preparations for his family's upcoming trip to South Carolina for the big reunion of his people. He talked back and forth with other barbers and clients who were telling stories of their elaborate reunions.

Social Affinity Networks

Social affinity networks organize around shared ideas, ideals, and causes. Such groups, ranging from neighborhood associations to national organizations, have played an important role in the lives of many African Americans. We highlight here several formal organizations developed by educated middle- and upper-middle-class Blacks. In each instance, the groups have both a social function and a larger mission to improve the lives of all African Americans.

The first type of group is the Black Greek Letter Organizations (BGLOs). These differ considerably in their history and focus from the Greek Letter Organizations (GLOs) known to most white college students. Both are secret, private societies out of the direct control of colleges and universities, but the similarities end there. Readers who are members of GLOs know the intricacies, but nonmembers are more likely to know only the bad behavior of fraternities—dangerous initiation practices, partying, binge drinking, and sexual misconduct (Marlene belonged to a sorority, Fern did not). Membership in GLOs is lifetime. Their greatest post-college advantage is the connections they can provide in opening the doors to professional and social opportunities. Most important for our purposes is the fact that the Greek system historically discriminated against non-whites by barring them from membership.

In response, Black students developed their own fraternities and sororities in the early 1900s. To show their priorities and distinctiveness, we focus on the first Black fraternity and sorority. The first Black fraternity, Alpha Phi Alpha, was organized at Cornell University in 1906. The founders stressed "manly deeds, scholarship, love for all mankind." Its objectives today, as listed on the website, are: "to stimulate the ambition of its members; to prepare them for the greatest usefulness in the causes of humanity, freedom, and dignity of the individual; to encourage the highest and noblest form of manhood; and to aid downtrodden humanity in its efforts to achieve higher social, economic and intellectual status." The website also describes the work of the fraternity: special initiatives that impact the African American community; national programs for mentoring, voter engagement, and elder care; and charitable work through several foundations.

The first Black sorority, Alpha Kappa Alpha, was founded in 1908 at Howard University. The founders believed that their status as educated women compelled them to address "an everlasting debt to raise them [the great mass of Negroes] up and to make them better." Today the organization focuses on two key priorities expressed on its website as: "the lifelong personal and professional development of each of its members; and galvanizing its membership into an organization of respected power and influence...at the forefront of effective advocacy and social change that results in equality and equity for all citizens of the world." In addition, "sisterly relations" stands as one of the organization's pillars: "it is that essential component...in which members intentionally take time apart to socialize and fellowship in order to create genuine bonds and connectedness that form lifelong relationships based on affinity, love, trust, respect and shared goals and interests."

As a result of being banned from affiliation with white fraternities and sororities, the five BGLOs in existence in 1930 formed the

National Pan-Hellenic Council. The number of BGLOs grew to nine, sometimes referred to as "the Divine Nine." They are all active today and differ from GLOs in allowing people to join after college graduation.

The BGLOs are distinctive for their history, which emphasized coming together to combat discrimination, and for their commitment to outreach and connection for the betterment of all people, with a focus on the needs of African Americans and other people of color. The networks and focused service of BGLOs are sustained by cultural values and practices embedded in their history and by mutual commitments to sustaining one another and bettering the lives of other Black people. Marlene maintains no contact with her sorority or any of the women who were in her campus chapter. We have a few white friends who are connected to people they met in their fraternity or sorority, but those friendships are in stark contrast to the relationships our Black friends have with members of their BGLOs. Black women refer to other Black women who were members of the same sorority, regardless of chapter or what years they were in college, as their "sisters." We know of countless experiences in which Black women have called on their "sisters" to help them professionally, to introduce them to other people who can help them professionally, and to advocate for them when they need help.

Another type of social affinity group brings together college educated and professional Black men and women. For example, Girl Friends, Inc., founded in 1927, and Links, Inc., founded in 1942, provide friendship and support for Black women. In addition, their members work to strengthen African American communities. The 100 Black Men of America, Inc., founded in 1963 in New York City, went national in 1986 with chapters throughout the US. They focus on African American youth, providing mentoring, education, economic empowerment, and health and wellness programs.

Clothing and Hair in African American Culture

The clothes we wear and style of our hair reflect both our personal preferences and cultural identity. An individual makes choices within their control about one type of clothing versus another, or one way to cut and comb one's hair versus another. Clothing and hair might reflect a person's choice to fit in or stand out, to conform or stand apart. Sometimes clothing and hair styles are prescribed for us, as is the case for those in the military. Sometimes they are constrained by norms, as in presenting oneself for a job interview. This section focuses on aspects of African American clothing and hair that are misunderstood by white people.

Clothing and Style

Although African Americans do not have a uniform style of dress, distinctive elements among many African Americans reflect cultural practices: the more formal attire of both men and women in professional settings, the stylish outfits worn by women for special occasions, African prints used in clothes for both men and women, the kente cloth stoles worn by college graduates, and the innovative clothing styles of musical artists that are often appropriated into broader style trends. Because the cultural meanings underlying clothing differ among groups, it's important for whites to better understand how the roots of their own practices differ from those of Blacks in America. Several examples illustrate the connection between what is visible and its cultural underpinnings.

Consider dressing up for church and the hats that some African American women wear. Christianity and its promise of a better life after death provided solace from the degradation of enslavement and lingering forms of racism. Worship provided a space for coming together, removed from the toil and stress of daily life. The tradition of dressing one's best for church demonstrated both respect for God and rejection of being seen as subhuman and ugly. Over time, dressing in Sunday best marked the clothing worn for church services: "To get decked out for church—suit, tie and pocket square for a man; stylish dress and coordinated hat for a woman—was to assert one's dignity as a citizen and one's value as a child of God."[23]

For some Black women, hats became an especially important part of Sunday dress—an expression of worth and respect and an homage to the headdresses worn by West African women. Because Black women would hold their heads high and carry themselves like queens when entering the church, the term "crown" became associated with their church hats. Helen Thomas of the Northwest African American Museum says the hats are "an expression of blackness and black culture that embodies self-expression, dignity, identity, tradition and respect."[24] The Sunday hat is less customary today, but still in fashion in some southern cities and among some older Black women.

Many white readers can relate to a dress code for worship services, but with a norm that emphasizes more subdued choices. Our mothers and grandmothers wore hats to church and synagogue, and our fathers wore suits, but they were not intended to call attention, except—for Christians—on Easter.

The more general pattern in Black culture of looking one's best conveys the same sense of racial pride and worth as does Sunday best. In professional and office settings, we often hear white women (men too) comment on Black women's sense of style and the well-dressed look of Black men. We've often said this ourselves. When whites do comment, it's important to remember the history and cultural traditions that underlie what we see.

In a very different cultural space than Sunday best attire, writers, intellectuals, singers, artists, and musicians of the Harlem Renaissance (post-World War I to 1929) brought innovative, dramatic styles into prominence. In Harlem venues, men wore three-piece suits, pocket squares, and leather wingtip shoes in contrasting black and white or black and brown. As the years went on, musicians moved to a looser style, which led to the zoot suits of the 1940s—long coats and oversized pants, often worn with porkpie or fedora hats. Women's styles were dramatic and looked expensive. Singers wore elaborate gowns and head adornments, and club attire for women included short dresses often in shimmering materials accessorized with long pearl necklaces, cloche hats, and feathered headbands.

Several decades later, hip-hop and rap culture introduced style trends that simultaneously appropriated and mocked luxury and created new ways to signify status. Africana Studies Professor Tricia Rose points to the succession of innovations rooted in the youth music scene: large fake diamond and gold jewelry and large designer emblems of the 70s and early 80s; the large plastic clock worn around the neck in the 80s; and the oversized pants, hoodies, and puffed-up down jackets of the 90s. Rapper Fred Brathwaite (aka Fab 5 Freddie) explained these innovations: "You make a new style. That's what life on the street is all about…honor and position on the street…a new style nobody can deal with."[25] These innovations crossed over into general culture and became fashion standards for white youth.

Interest in African design and style also began to appear during the civil rights era. Dashiki shirts for men contrasted sharply with standard men's attire: "brightly colored instead of drab, loose instead of tight, worn outside the pants instead of tucked in…worn defiantly for occasions that generally call for a coat and tie."[26] Women also adopted dashiki prints for tops, outfits, and dresses, and men and women alike started to wear the long Senegalese-style kaftans. The most authentic garments display color and meaning through kente cloth, originally woven by the Ashanti people of Ghana. In the early 1990s, Black students began to wear kente cloth graduation stoles as a symbol of heritage and accomplishment.

Hair and Heritage

Most white people know little about the hair of African Americans, unless we have had intimate relationships or close family or friendship ties with African Americans. We vividly recall the day we attended a workshop focused on hair care for white parents of Black children. When we arrived, a Black beautician was vigorously combing through the tight curls in a Black girl's hair. The girl was sobbing but also being comforted by the beautician. The girl's white mother looked on horrified. The beautician pointed out that the child's hair had not been "taken care of" and that her white parent needed to learn the daily routine of combing so that the girl would be seen as properly cared for. Fern remembered the snarls in her long hair when she was a child, wiggling and crying as her mother combed through her hair before braiding or putting it in a ponytail. Yet she knew that what she was seeing didn't match her experience. What was different? Put simply, "the hair."

"Afro-textured hair," which occurs in African populations, the African diaspora, and parts of South and Southeast Asia, appears denser and thicker because each strand grows "in a tiny, angle-like helix shape."[27] African Americans have different texture types and degrees of hair coiling, especially because of the degree of Black-white mixed heritage going back to enslavement, but it is uncommon for white people to have hair that is coiled and helix-like. Similarly, the straight black hair of Asian peoples is rarely seen in the white population.

Historically, the pressures to conform to white beauty standards in the US led Black people to straighten their hair with hot combs and irons, and later with harsh chemicals. Marita Golden recounts her childhood experiences sitting for hours in the kitchen while her mother straightened her hair with a hot iron: "What happened to me in my mother's kitchen was part of the generations-old tradition and requirement in the Black community. For women and men to be accepted by and successful in both the Black and the White worlds, we had to look, either through hair texture, skin color, or phenotype, like Whites. Of the three, hair texture has always been the easiest to change."[28] Think of all the shampoo ads that show white women swinging their long flowing hair, often in slow motion. Up through the 1960s, Black men also straightened their hair into the conk style, using a lye product.

Although hair straightening is still done and the methods improved, the practice tapered off with the rise of the Black pride and Black is Beautiful movements of the 1960s and 70s. That era gave birth to the Afro and its association with African heritage. Angela Davis, political activist and academic, famously wore a large Afro as a statement of Black pride, as did many members of the Black Panther Party. The Afro signified political revolution and cultural pride in African heritage and rejected the imposition of white standards.

Personal Prompt: List problems you have with your hair. For example, is it too curly or too straight, does it lack body or shine? Take your list to the store where you typically buy hair products. Do they have products that help with your hair problems? Now check the shelves for products designed for Black hair. Do you see any? Where are they placed? Are there many choices? Think about the implications of your findings.

The Afro ushered in a range of other hair styles that honor cultural heritage: varieties of cornrows, dreadlocks, extensions, weaves, twists, braiding. Writing in *Essence* (a lifestyle magazine for Black women), Siraad Dirshe describes braids as "an inextricable part of Black culture. We have carried these styles with us throughout history—from Africa to southern plantations to northern inner-city salons and beyond.... Not only do we proudly opt to wear our braids, but we also reclaim them— time and time again—as our birthright and that of our ancestors."[29]

Along with all these changes in hair styles, wigs remain part of daily life for many African American women. When a white woman wears a wig, it's most likely because she has thin hair or substantial hair loss from arena alopecia (an autoimmune condition), female-pattern hair loss, various medical conditions, or chemotherapy. Black women have two additional reasons. First is how much time and effort it takes to style and nourish Afro-textured hair. Wigs save time and help protect the hair. One writer explains that a wig is "a great protective style to help my natural hair thrive, maintain length, and be healthier in general. It gives my hair a breather from the constant styling my natural hair requires."[30] Second is traction alopecia (technically known as central centrifugal cicatricial alopecia, or CCCA). Dr. Crystal Aguh, a Black dermatologist specializing in ethnic hair loss, defines its cause: "heat, chemicals and tight styles that pull at the hair root, including some braids, dreadlocks, extensions and weaves."[31]

The movement to affirm the cultural heritage of Black hair started over a half century ago, yet white people still exotify, malign, and police Black hair. Most whites do not want strangers or casual acquaintances asking, "Can I touch your hair?" or, worse, just putting their fingers on our hair. But this happens to Black people all the time as white people wonder what Black hair might feel like. We can't begin to count how many times this happened to our sons when they were young and still happens to them as adults. The only explanation is that whites see Black hair as exotic and do not understand that hair touching is a microaggression.

The maligning of Black hair comes in the form of verbal aggressions. These might be comments about a Black woman's "weird" hairdo or the design cut into a Black man's hair. Derogatory terms for Black hair still exist, with the most long-standing and charged adjectives being "nappy," and "nappy-headed." These are complicated terms dating from the slave trade, but their power to denigrate remains today. Some readers might recall the 2007 cancellation of Don Imus's CBS radio talk show *Imus in the Morning* after he called the Rutgers women's basketball team "nappy-headed hos." Yes, Black people do use the word "nappy," which can be confusing to whites (but likely wasn't to Don Imus). When Blacks use "nappy," they are reclaiming a term to give it a new and positive meaning. When a white person uses the term, it's a cultural misappropriation to be avoided.

The policing of Black hair continues to be in the news. When schools and workplaces ban or set guidelines that exclude hair styles common among Black people, they are policing cultural practices that are important to their users. Whether motivated by insensitivity, lack of understanding, or racism, such policies appear intended to control Black bodies. For example, in 2020, a school in Texas suspended a Black student for wearing his hair in dreadlocks and told him that he couldn't participate in graduation unless he cut his hair. Why? Ostensibly because there was a school policy about long hair. Yet the student had been wearing dreadlocks for several years.[32] At the end of an extensive story about the incident on *CBS This Morning*, Gayle King, the African American host, said, "In the Black culture, your hair, dreadlocks are acceptable...not an unusual hairdo."[33] In late 2018, a white referee told a

Black high school wrestler in New Jersey to cut off his dreadlocks or forfeit his match—despite official rules allowing head covers.[34] He didn't want to forfeit so he stood there as a team trainer cut off his dreads. Outrage erupted. The referee was eventually suspended for two years. In 2014, the US Army banned cornrows, twists, and dreadlocks. They reversed the decision after massive protest, including pressure from the Congressional Black Caucus. In a story about a variety of hair policing cases, a Black Los Angeles lawyer wrote: "We shouldn't feel compelled to conform to a grooming standard that mandates we suppress our cultural roots and identity. Instead, we should expect and demand to be judged by our performance and the strength of our ideas."[35]

The frequent cases of hair policing in schools and workplaces led three states to enact legislation to ban the practice. California's 2018 Crown Act, which stands for "Create a Respectful and Open Workplace for Natural Hair," prohibits discrimination based on hair style and texture. New York and New Jersey have passed similar legislation.[36]

White people need to understand that hair care and styling are cultural and that hair remains a site of misunderstanding and racism for Black men and women. There's a telling scene in an episode of NBC's *This Is Us* in which Kevin, a white man, is dating a Black woman. They are several hours into a road trip when she realizes that she has forgotten her silk pillowcase. She is visibly upset, and he tries to minimize her concern, making it clear that he thinks she wants the pillowcase because she prefers to sleep on silk. After they arrive at their hotel, she calls her best friend, a Black woman, and says, "How can I be with a man who doesn't understand why I need my pillowcase?" Many Black women sleep on silk pillowcases to help prevent split ends and breakage, which Black hair is prone to. Some Black men and women also wear a scarf, called a "durag" or "do-rag," to bed to keep their hair frizz-free and maintain their hair pattern.[37] In the 1990s, some Black hip-hoppers, rappers, entertainers, and urban male teenagers began wearing the do-rag in public as a statement of cultural identity. Many whites associated this trend with criminality and urban gangs. More recently, prominent Black entertainers and athletes wear do-rags, often with innovative style. We now see some white entertainers and fashion designers appropriating the trend as a fashion statement, likely without understanding its function in maintaining Black hair.

Most whites don't know about silk pillowcases and do-rags. This lack of knowledge often leads to not only misinterpretations but also demeaning judgments about Blacks.

Moving the Conversation Forward

This chapter examined some of the many cultural practices associated with African Americans. Our intent is to encourage greater cultural mindedness and interest in the origin and significance of cultural practices that differ from those of most whites. Clearly, more cross-race conversation will help whites get a better understanding of aspects of Black culture that they misinterpret or know nothing about.

Things Not to Do

- If a Black friend complains about their dry hair, don't say, "I know what you mean. My hair is dry too." Blacks have unique issues. Recognize them. You can find common ground in complaining about your hair or skin, but not by assuming your hair and skin are comparable to your Black friend's. Instead, ask how your friend maintains their hair.
- Don't lump all Black people into the same category, cultural or otherwise. Don't make statements like "Black people support Joe Biden for President rather than Cory Booker." Instead, say, "I've noticed that some polls suggest that a majority of Blacks support Biden," or "Many Black voters appear to prefer Biden to other candidates." Many years ago, when Marlene was a graduate student, another student asked her, "How do Jews vote?" Luckily one of Marlene's friends, also Jewish, was present and quickly replied, "In voting booths." Everyone laughed, defusing a potentially fraught moment.
- Don't say "You people," "You're different from the others," or "You're so articulate." They're offensive. Period.

- Don't try to talk the way you think a Black person talks. It's offensive, even if you think your motive for doing so is positive, for example, you think that "sounding Black" is cool. What you're doing is an affectation. It's not genuine.

Things to Do

- If you're unsure about a cultural practice or whether something you've observed is culturally based, take responsibility for learning about it on your own. For example, some Blacks include the tradition of "jumping the broom" in their wedding ceremony. The bride and groom jump over a broom signifying a new beginning and sweeping away the past. The tradition also pays respect to enslaved ancestors who—disallowed from legal marriage—jumped a broom to show their commitment. If you hear a reference to "jumping the broom," a Google search yields an explanation.
- When someone comments negatively about AAE or any other African American cultural practice, ask first why they think that. If they say it's a fact, try to offer some basic information. If they say it's an opinion, explore how that opinion can be harmful to Black people.
- When the opportunity arises, comment about the tendency for whites to misunderstand or say demeaning things about Black cultural practices.
- Access news sources and lifestyle media directed to the Black audience, for example magazines and news sources (over 200 African American-owned community papers are members of the National Newspaper Publishers Association, which also sponsors Black Press USA—an online news source); the Oprah Winfrey Channel (OWN); and the new Black News Channel (BNC). Talk with other white people about what you read and watch and mention these sources when the topic is relevant.

Chapter 6

Better Talk

Putting It All Together

THE PREVIOUS CHAPTERS EXPLAIN why talking about race is critical for moving our country forward, why white people avoid or don't want to talk about race, and the gaps whites have in our knowledge of Black history, culture, and everyday life. They provide the foundation for having more productive conversations about race, both with other white people and across race. In this chapter we discuss ways to structure conversations about race, how talk can lead to action, and where to find other people with whom to have those conversations. Our hope is that the preceding information and ideas will form the basis of those conversations. We also offer suggestions for where you can find additional resources in your search for information and ideas about race.

The first section of this chapter identifies ways to structure conversations about race that allow people to engage with each other with honesty and depth and to continue talking even when the conversations are uncomfortable or hurtful. Several years ago, when we were facilitating a conversation about race, we asked participants if we had missed any guidelines they thought important for structuring the discussion. A Black woman in the group said, "Take courage." She was right to add courage to our list. Whether you are white or a person of color, it takes enormous courage to open yourself up to others to talk about race. Whites have to confront, often for the first time, the reality of the privileges we have simply because of the color of our skin. Blacks have to agree to share their pain and anger when they know that whites may not always immediately understand the depth of that pain and anger. That you have made it this far in the book and are ready to begin talking suggests you have the courage to engage in productive conversations about race.

Guidelines for Engagement

Conversations are governed by rules. Most of us could not say what those rules are because, like much of our knowledge about culture, the rules are tacit. We know them simply because we've grown up in this culture and have learned them through trial and error. The only time we're aware of conversational rules is when someone breaks one. For example, we take turns in conversation because conversation is understood to be back-and-forth, not a monologue. If one person keeps interrupting another or "holds the floor" for too long, we might say, "Hey, give me a chance to say something."

Because conversations about race are both difficult and potentially dangerous for people, our tacit rules about conversation are not sufficient. We need explicit guidelines about how to structure our conversations so that everyone feels safe and free to speak. We prefer to call the rules of engagement in conversations about race "guidelines" rather than rules. "Rules" implies rigidity, and our hope for these conversations is that they are fluid rather than static, spontaneous rather than rehearsed. The guidelines are not unique to conversations about race. They can be used in any difficult conversations. The guidelines are also not unique to us as authors. You will find similar guidelines in many books and articles about dialogue. Here we highlight the ones that we believe are most essential to productive talk about race. Feel free in your conversations to ask participants to suggest additional guidelines.

The three young Black feminists who started the #BlackLivesMatter movement, Alicia Garza, Patrisse Cullors, and Opal Tometi, posit four general guidelines for talking about race: lead with love, low ego, high impact, and move at the speed of trust.[1] These guidelines capture several concepts that we've discussed previously—the importance of not being defensive ("it's not all about you"), the necessity of building trust, and the importance of having empathy for other people. These guidelines point to an additional concept: high impact. In other words, productive conversations about race focus on significant ideas, and they make a difference in the lives of the participants. They transform our personal understanding, create new relationships, lead to concrete individual and/or group action, or any combination of these.

The set of guidelines we use in our own work are based on those initially used in the Boston City-Wide Dialogues on Racial and Ethnic Diversity, a series of neighborhood-based, multi-session, facilitated conversations about race. These dialogues were launched in late 2003 by the Urban League of Eastern Massachusetts; endorsed by the Office of the Mayor and numerous racial, ethnic, and religious groups throughout the city; and funded by grants from major private foundations in the city. Facilitators were volunteers with prior group facilitation experience, and participants were recruited on a voluntary basis. Marlene worked with the project from the beginning and continued as a facilitator after it was absorbed into YW Boston (formerly the YWCA) and renamed the YW Boston Dialogues on Race and Ethnicity. The original curriculum, including dialogue guidelines, was developed by Cheryl Harris, head of Cheryl Harris & Associates, a change management consulting group, and Rebecca Shuster, who was then Director of Training at the Massachusetts Commission Against Discrimination and is now the Assistant Superintendent of Equity for the Boston Public Schools. Harris is African American and Shuster is white. The curriculum was based on several existing dialogue models, such as those used by the National Conference for Communities and Justice, Study Circles Resource Center, One America, and the Anti-Defamation League's World of Difference program.

The guidelines we list here are adapted from those used by YW Boston. As we identify each guideline, you'll see how they relate to points we've made earlier about how to participate in conversations about race.

- *Be engaged and present.* We can all relate to the experience of being in a conversation but not being fully present. We might be thinking about an argument we had with our spouse/ partner that morning or a project we must finish at work or the pain we're feeling in our knees after biking yesterday. To participate in a conversation about race, we need to be fully present. We need to pay close attention to what people are saying and how they're saying it. And we need to ensure that we hear everything in its full context, not just snatches of conversation as our mind wanders in and out.

- *Maintain confidentiality.* Trust is critical to conversations about race. Honest talk about race requires that participants feel secure that others in the conversation will not talk about them outside of the conversation. For example, if I risk saying something that shows my ignorance about Black history or experience, I want to know that what I say stays in the conversation. If a Black person shares a personal experience about discrimination, they want to know that what they share with you will not be broadcast to others without their permission. Agree to learn from each other and share the ideas you learn with others, but don't talk about individual people or reveal personal information that can be attached to individuals.

- *Be respectful and welcoming.* No blaming, shaming, or dismissing. No racial slurs or other offensive words or phrases. No personal attacks. Remember to "lead with love," which means that we strive to hear what others have to say, enhance understanding, and move forward constructively.

- *Share the conversation.* Taking turns is fundamental to conversation. As we said earlier, conversations are dialogues, not monologues. Agree to share the speaking time. Some people like to talk, and others tend to be quieter, sometimes because they're shy, sometimes because they need time to think about what's being said. Set some guidelines for how to share talk time. You can give people a set amount of time to speak. You can insist that a new person speak each time until everyone has had a chance to speak and then begin the process again. Also, be mindful that Blacks have been marginalized historically in conversations with whites. You can use your conversations about race to disrupt that pattern. Establish a practice of having a Black person or other person of color begin the conversation, but do not do this to put a person of color on the spot. Ask that whites defer to Blacks when several people want to take a turn at the same time. Also set some guidelines for how to deal with interruptions. Interruptions are natural in conversation, but they often lead to domination by one person or group of people, and they become a way to silence others. For example, linguistic studies show that men frequently interrupt both women and other men. Women, on the other hand, are less likely to interrupt, which means that they are often silenced in mixed conversations. And because historically women have deferred to men, they will often allow men to dominate the conversation. The same is true in mixed-race conversations, where Blacks are interrupted by whites and where Blacks have historically been marginalized. Correcting this problem means having clear guidelines about not interrupting. You can establish a practice of allowing people to speak without interruption except for clarifying questions from others. For example, if someone is describing an interaction with a police officer and you're not sure where the incident happened, you can ask a question. But you cannot interrupt to say, "That happened to me too" or "I can't believe that happened to you."

- *Speak from your own experience.* Your experience, your "truth," and your reality may differ from or even be opposite to someone else's. Share your truth and be open to hearing others' truths. Most of us learn best from our own experiences or by hearing other people's stories. Ideas become real when they are explored through experience rather than theory. In chapter 3, we talked about coming to truly understand white privilege only after we adopted our sons, even though we had both taught the concept for many years. That was a life-changing experience, just as many experiences that happen through conversation can completely change how we think about something—in this case, how we think about race.

- *Use "I" statements to qualify your comments.* Saying "I believe" or "I feel" when you are offering your opinions helps to condition your comments so that others do not become defensive and makes you—rather than someone else—responsible for the comment. Avoid saying "many people think" or "other people believe." We have no way to verify the truthfulness of the statement, but inserting it into the conversation sounds like the speaker is trying to give it credibility without taking responsibility for it.

- *Embrace disagreements.* Disagreements are productive. Different opinions about an issue usually point to different experiences related to that issue. Think back to chapter 4 and consider the different assessments Blacks and whites have about the police. Those judgements are based on people's experiences with the police, sometimes directly through real experiences, sometimes mediated through television, film, the internet, or other media. Rather than walk away from disagreements, embrace them. Ask the person who disagrees with you why they believe what they believe. Do this to better understand the person's position, not to interrogate them about their beliefs. A conversation is not a debate. We're not looking for winners and losers. We're looking to increase our understanding.

- *Consider your intent and impact.* We assume everyone participating in the conversation means well. As the Black Lives Matter guidelines say, we "lead with love." But even the best intentions can go awry. A well-meaning comment, gesture, or facial expression can still hurt someone else. Marlene was facilitating a dialogue session in which participants, including the facilitators, shared an object that reflected their identity. Marlene shared a picture of our family and talked about her identity as a member of an interracial family. After the session, several participants of color objected. What they heard was Marlene saying she has a Black identity, a claim they found personally insulting and hurtful. Marlene's intent was not to deny her white identity and its privileges but rather to say that being a member of an interracial family made her more aware of the privileges she has and our children do not have. But her intent didn't matter. Her impact did. She listened to the feedback, apologized to the group at the next session, and explained her point more clearly. As speakers in a conversation about race, we need to hold ourselves accountable for the impact of our words and actions. It's not enough to say, "I didn't intend to hurt you." As listeners in the conversation, we need to both assume good intentions on the part of the other participants and hold ourselves accountable for speaking up when we hear or see something that we find hurtful. Some groups use the practice of saying "ouch" when something hurtful is said. The person who says "ouch" then has the responsibility to explain why. The group can then use the interchange as a teachable moment. We learn why our words or actions are hurtful to others in a way that allows us to build trust with each other and continue the conversation. If the "ouch technique" does not feel right, other signals can be used—a hand gesture, saying "pause," and so forth.

Talk Versus Action

As teachers and facilitators, we often hear people say that they are tired of talking about race. They want to know when we're going to do something to make racial conflict and disparities go away. As a culture, Americans are quick to jump to solutions, to want action before we've taken time to understand problems fully. Our desire to move quickly often leads to poor policy decisions, ones that don't address the underlying causes of the problem we're trying to solve or ones that have unintended consequences that exacerbate the original problem.

The Violent Crime Control and Law Enforcement Act of 1994 provides an example. Hastily put together by the Clinton administration for a variety of political reasons and widely supported by both Democrats and Republicans (including the Congressional Black Caucus), the act is now seen as a major contributor to the overcrowding of US prisons and the mass incarceration of Black and Latinx men. By increasing police presence on urban streets, the act did help lessen violent crime (although violent crime was already on the decline by 1994), but it also provided stiffer penalties for drug-related crimes and gave states money to build prisons if they passed "truth in sentencing" laws that required convicted criminals to serve at least 85% of their sentences. Further, the law mandated "three strikes and you're out" for all federal crimes, giving judges no leeway to lessen sentences for lesser crimes. Each of these provided the impetus for states to increase the number of prisons and prisoners.

Knowing how to solve problems requires fully understanding the underlying causes of the problems. Thinking back to 1994, talking with people in communities of color, lawyers and judges, social workers, medical professionals, and others might have revealed the likely consequences of the policies in the Violent Crime Control and Law Enforcement Act. Remember the consequences for Black and brown men of the disparate sentencing for possession of crack versus powder cocaine that we detailed in chapter 4.

Policies and actions are generally improved if the people who are most affected by those policies and actions are involved in both the discussions and the decisions about what is needed. Both of us have been involved in conversations with other white people in situations where we have all been trying to figure out ways to involve more people of color in groups in which we participate. For example, how do we get more parents of color at PTO meetings or hire more faculty of color at our universities? All of the whites in these conversations have been well-intentioned, but they have often been clueless about the experiences of people of color. When Marlene first started facilitating Boston City-Wide Dialogues, the project focused on bringing together racially diverse groups of people who lived in particular neighborhoods. At the first meeting, participants would pledge to attend all of the sessions. But Marlene noticed that Black and Latinx participants often missed sessions or arrived noticeably late. When she commented on what appeared to be a pattern of less commitment on the part of participants of color, her co-facilitator, who was Black, gently pointed out that the people who were late or absent had family responsibilities in the evening and no resources to pay for help or took public transportation, which is frequently not on time or broken-down in Boston. Marlene took the lesson to heart, reminding herself not to make judgements about people without knowing their personal circumstances. And the people working with the Dialogues had to rethink how to schedule the sessions and support people who had difficulty attending in the evening.

Talk is also important because it lays the foundation for purposeful action and relationships. Being able to talk about race, especially with people of another race, is essential for forming genuine cross-racial friendships. An African American friend recently said that she was beginning to rethink her friendships with white people. She works in a predominantly white organization and has always had many white friends, not just work friends but people who also have dinner at her home and spend time with her husband and children. She said that talking about race was an important part of her friendships with other Black people, but she had recently realized that she never talks about race with her white friends other than us. She said they either avoid the subject or deflect from discussions about race if she raises the topic. She said she felt as if her white friends didn't really know her, and she was beginning to question if they were, indeed, real friends.

People want to be known to others, to share their stories with other people. We have both been struck by how much people talk when they are asked about themselves. Contemporary society leaves many of us disconnected from others. Whether it's because of the culture wars, the fractured nature of our politics, or the myriad ways that technology removes us from face-to-face contact with others, people seem to crave genuine connection. Conversations about race can provide that connection and give all of us an opportunity to know others and be known to them in ways that can nourish real friendships. These friendships also create the trust that is necessary for people to work together productively.

If we hope to create a more equitable social union, we need to build trust among people both locally and nationally. Loose coalitions of individuals or groups trying to achieve short-term goals do not create long-term, fundamental structural change. Deep structural change requires more.

Finding Conversational Partners

Some people have natural groups that they can call on for starting conversations about race. For example, if you are a member of a book group, you can suggest that the group read a work of fiction or nonfiction by a Black author that will prompt a discussion of Black life. The book can explore historical or contemporary issues. Many churches, synagogues, mosques, and other religious organizations have formed racial equity groups or are a natural place to find people interested in creating such a group.

You can also create a group of your own by asking neighbors, friends, or co-workers to join you in a discussion of race. A friend used Facebook's "Red Table Talk" show as a model to create a group devoted to conversations about significant and often difficult topics, including race. Red Table Talk is a concept created by the actor Jada Pinkett Smith, who brought together her daughter, Willow Smith, and her mother, Adrienne Banfield Norris ("Gammy"), to create an intergenerational conversation group. They took their conversation to Facebook TV, where they interview celebrities about serious topics such as gender identity, drug addiction, and race. Our friend asked friends who span several generations to have similar discussions.

Finding mixed-race groups to talk with is more difficult. Black British writer Reni Eddo-Lodge, author of *Why I'm No Longer Talking to White People About Race*, declared in a 2014 blog post, "I can no longer engage with the gulf of an emotional disconnect that white people display when a person of colour articulates their experience."[2] We know many people of color who say they're tired of educating whites and no longer want to talk about race with them. Others say they don't trust whites or don't believe that whites are genuine when they talk about race. The biggest obstacle to finding mixed race groups, however, is that we live in separate neighborhoods and live separate lives.

One way to start is to spend time in neighborhoods of color. You can attend community events, plays, lectures, or musical events. Or go shopping in a predominantly Black neighborhood, where you will find lots of stores carrying clothing and other goods that are not available where you usually shop. If you generally attend church, find a church in a Black community that welcomes visitors and attend. But don't go once or twice; go often enough that people begin to recognize you. Greet people, not only in church but in the stores or walking along the street. Don't wait for others to initiate with you. Blacks may be suspicious about why you're there. Even in predominantly Black spaces, whites hold power and may be seen as threatening. If you feel out of place, remember that Black people enter situations all the time where they are seen as the "other."

We give this suggestion—to spend time in Black neighborhoods—with a caveat. There is a fine line between genuine reaching out to and participating in a community and simply being a tourist. In recent years, Black churches, especially in Harlem, have become destinations for white tourists from around the world, generally because travel agents and guidebooks recommend them as sites for hearing gospel music. Whites flock to them, often arriving in tour buses, seeking entertainment. Lloyd Williams, president of the Harlem Chamber of Commerce, explained to a white journalist that it's like whites are on a safari and "we're the zebras."[3] Whites who spend time in communities of color need to do so as participants who have a real stake in those communities, not as spectators or tourists in a foreign country.

You can do other things. Look for community-based dialogues on race that attract people of different backgrounds or community groups that form around issues related to race and ethnicity. Often communities will call for public discussions of race. Mayor Marty Walsh of Boston, for example, called for a dialogue on race in his 2015 inauguration speech. He has followed through with annual community dialogues that draw together hundreds of people. As we noted in chapter 1, these "dialogues" are not true conversations—there's little back and forth interaction—but they are opportunities to hear from people about their experiences and to learn from them. We recently attended a local community forum in which three young Black men who had been incarcerated for different reasons talked about their experiences in prison and how they've managed to integrate back into the community. Although we didn't speak at the session or even ask a question, we gained new insights into racial disparities in the criminal justice system.

Similar to these forums, audience "talk backs" after theater performances provide an opportunity to hear from people in the community. Pick a play about race by a Black playwright, attend the performance, and stay for the discussion. Or pick a play by a white playwright that looks at issues related to race and being white. For example, Joshua Harmon's *Admissions* explores what happens when progressive white parents who work at a private high school find out that their son didn't get into his first-choice college while his best friend, who is Black, did. When possible, pick a theater that attracts Black audiences.

Another way to begin to engage with Blacks is through The Race Card Project (TRCP). Conceived by African American journalist Michelle Norris, TRCP asks people to write a six-word essay about race and post it online at theracecardproject.com. Again, there's no face-to-face talk about race, but you do have the opportunity to learn about the experiences and ideas of others. The technique can be adapted for use in a conversational group.

Creating an interracial face-to-face conversation may take more ingenuity, especially if you don't have a wide circle of friends, neighbors, or co-workers of color. If you have one or a few Black friends, you could ask if they would be willing to engage with you about race. Keep in mind, however, that you cannot ask them to speak for all Black people. Each of us can speak only for ourselves as we share experiences, ideas, opinions, etc. Be sure, therefore, that you let your conversational partner know that you are not asking them to speak for others, but only for themselves.

Cheryle Moses, a Black woman in Lawrenceville, Georgia, decided to invite people to a networking event called Come Meet a Black Person.[4] She got the idea for the event when she read that whites rarely have Black friends and Blacks rarely have white friends. Her hope is that bringing whites and Blacks together in the same space to network with each other will lead to talk about how to work toward eliminating racism.

Two women in Denver, Colorado, came up with a unique way of bringing other women together to talk about race. Regina Jackson, who is Black, and Saira Rao, who is Indian American, created the Race to Dinner project, in which they advertise for liberal white women who can pay $2,500 each to have dinner with them to talk about racism and the power that white women have to dismantle it.[5] We're not suggesting that others do a similar project. But the idea of asking people to come together over supper to talk about race resonates for us. If you think there are some like-minded people in your church, your PTO, your office, your neighborhood, or any other group you are part of, you could send out an invitation to join together over a meal to talk about race. Many of us come from cultural traditions in which breaking bread together is a way to build bridges across differences. Talk over a meal offers rich possibilities for opening up genuine conversations about our differences while we also discover our similarities.

Jackson and Rao offer advice that is worth thinking about as you seek out others for conversation. They say that they target liberal white women because they believe it's possible to get them to recognize their role in maintaining systemic racism and to do something to effect change. They say that white men and women who voted for Donald Trump, however, are not open to their message. Their advice echoes the work of several authors who have studied rural white Americans in the aftermath of the 2016 election. Jonathan M. Metzl,[6] Francesco

Duina,[7] and Robert Wuthnow[8] each interviewed rural whites who supported Trump. Each author focuses on different aspects of their interviewees' opposition to government policies that would improve their economic and physical well-being, but all ultimately agree that the core of their opposition is their determination to hold onto their race privilege, to their vision of a world in which white men dominate. We cannot help all white people see racism, especially systemic racism, or help them understand that we are all complicit in maintaining racism. Seek out people who seem genuinely interested in talking about race, who at least say they want to learn and are open to listening. But know that not everyone will be.

Resources

There are numerous ways that you can learn more about the lives and experiences of people of color so that you are able to participate in informed discussions about race. As suggested in chapter 5, accessing media designed for people of color is a starting point. In the mid-2000s, Marlene taught a media class in which her college students teamed up with a group of Boston high school students of color to study coverage of communities of color in the Boston area by the *Boston Globe*. Not surprisingly, they found little to no coverage except of Black politicians, sports figures, entertainers, or people accused of crimes. There was virtually no coverage of other individuals or communities of color even though Boston has robust Asian and Latinx communities. When Marlene's students asked the high school students to suggest stories they would like to see in the newspaper, they said they wanted everyone to know more about who they were, where they lived, and what they experienced. Except in times of devastating events, such as Hurricane Katrina, the coronavirus pandemic, and the current racial crisis accelerated by the killing of George Floyd, the media that most whites turn to rarely cover issues directly about or related to the experiences of people of color. Broadening your media consumption to include sources important to people of color provides a different and essential perspective as you begin to talk about race.

We identified some of these sources in chapter 5. Again, most major US cities have Black newspapers, and the Black News Channel is now available in some cable markets and online.

Black radio is also a great source of information, especially about Black culture. A Google search will yield a list of the top 10 African American-influenced radio stations. These give you access primarily to music that is African American-influenced, much of which whites are now familiar with because African American music has been incorporated into mainstream American music. Across the US, there are 335 Black radio stations. Most whites are unfamiliar with the important role these stations played in US history. During the civil rights movement in the 1960s, they encouraged listeners to go to rallies, using secret codes that avoided tipping off the police, and also alerted listeners to where the police might have set up blockades.[9] These stations also broke down racial barriers as they drew in white listeners during the late 20th century.

To learn more about Black experience, you can read fiction, nonfiction, and poetry by Black authors and read or attend plays by Black playwrights. We provide suggestions online at **www.letstalkrace.com**.

Many websites offer suggestions for how to organize dialogues about race; some also provide resources for whites who want to learn more about Black life and experience. You can find many more online, but here are three that will get you started.

- The Southern Poverty Law Center website section on teaching tolerance includes resources for elementary and high school teachers. The information is also valuable for individuals seeking more information about Black history and contemporary life. **splccenter.org/teaching-tolerance**
- Facing History and Ourselves provides resources for educators looking for ways to address racism, antisemitism, and prejudice. The website includes a wealth of historical information along with ideas for ways to connect history to our present-day lives. **facinghistory.org**

- The Black Lives Matter website provides a toolkit for white people, including conversation starters and other information. **blacklivesmatter.com**

Moving the Conversation Forward

Things Not to Do

- Throughout this book, we have given you suggestions for how to have more productive conversations with other people about race, including suggestions for talking with Blacks about race. Some of those suggestions include speaking up when other whites say or imply something racist or racially insensitive, or ensuring that Blacks are centered in the conversation or have opportunities to speak without interruption. Do these things. But don't expect to be thanked or applauded for doing them. They're your responsibility, not your good deeds. *The Revisioners: A Novel* by Margaret Wilkerson Sexton tells a multigenerational story about Ava, a young mixed-race woman in New Orleans in 2017 and her great-great-grandmother, Josephine, a former slave who goes on to become a landowner and run the family farm. The story explores the racial divide through each woman's experiences at different points in time. One telling moment occurs in 1924 when Josephine is talking with her neighbor, Charlotte, a young white woman, after Josephine's son and daughter-in-law are terrorized by the KKK. Charlotte and her husband are members of the KKK, and he was with the Klansmen the night they terrorized Josephine's family. Charlotte tells Josephine that she confronted her husband about what he had done, and he beat her for speaking up. Josephine responds, "I'm sorry about that…. Nobody deserves that." Josephine then describes what happens next: "There is silence then. I can tell she expects more from me, applause maybe for what she has given up, taken on my behalf."[10] But Josephine isn't going to give her that applause. Whatever Charlotte has "given up" or endured on Josephine's behalf is nothing compared to what Josephine endures every day. As white people, we have a responsibility to speak up in the face of racism; we don't need or deserve anyone's thanks for doing so.

- Don't ask a Black person to speak for all Black people. As we said earlier, use "I" statements when you are offering an opinion or idea. You can only speak for yourself, not for others. So, don't expect Blacks to speak for other Blacks. Most Blacks in the US can recount the many times that people, especially teachers, have pointed to them, often when they were the only Black person in the room, and asked them, "How do Black people feel/think about X?" By asking a single Black person to speak for all Black people, we erase the diversity and breadth of Black experiences. The group and the individual are not identical, and one cannot stand in for the other.

- Don't expect Black people to be noncombative in conversations with whites. *Boston Globe* editorial writer Renee Graham recounted a conversation Jackie Robinson had with Branch Rickey, Brooklyn Dodgers' president and owner, shortly before he asked Robinson to join the Dodgers as the first African American player in Major League Baseball. Rickey told Robinson he knew he was a good ballplayer, but he didn't know if he had "guts enough not to fight back."[11] Graham argued that "in a racist system, challenging racism is deemed worse than racism," and she concluded that being asked to have the guts not to fight back, or to go high when others go low, as former First Lady Michelle Obama famously said, exacts too great an emotional and psychological price from Blacks. We applaud Obama's entreaty, but agree with Graham. Whites need to give Blacks the space to vent, to fight back against racism, and we need to be willing to take the blows by listening and hearing the anger and pain that are the culmination of centuries of racist abuse. In a review of James McBride's novel *Deacon King Kong*, Junot Diaz, who like

McBride is a man of color, wrote that people of African descent have endured "an infinity of suffering": "What lingers after the last page of this terrific novel is not laughter or thunderbolts or the endless resilience of communities of color but something far more unsettling: grief, like the sound of many waters, wide, dark, deep."[12]

- Don't expect or aim for perfection. We live in an age in which technology lets us present a perfect face to the world. Whether it's through creating perfect pictures of ourselves and others through Photoshop or curating the stories we tell about ourselves on Facebook and Instagram, we've come to expect perfection. But as we've said many times in this book, conversations about race are messy and difficult. We all make mistakes, say something we wish we hadn't said, or embarrass ourselves by revealing our ignorance. Unlike writing on a computer where we can hit the Delete key when we realize we've made a mistake, we can't take back our words in conversation. But we can apologize for them and admit that we're not perfect. Aim for being authentic rather than perfect.

- Don't expect to feel good after a conversation about race. Often you will feel bad, perhaps because you said or did something hurtful or embarrassing, perhaps because the conversation reached an impasse and you couldn't find a way forward, perhaps because you were overwhelmed by guilt, perhaps because you thought others in the conversation didn't like you or were suspicious of you, or perhaps because you were angry. Conversations about race are not necessarily feel-good times. You may feel good because you know you're doing the right thing, but still feel bad—about yourself, about the conversation, about other people. Think about why you're feeling bad. Gaining some insight might help you feel better about the conversation. Or it might not. In either case, keep moving forward.

Things to Do

- Start—now. It's hard to take the first step and even harder to put ourselves out there, to make ourselves vulnerable to others. But we have to do that if we expect to move the conversation on race forward and begin the healing that is necessary to move the country forward. The conversations will be difficult and even painful, but we have to start. Remember what a participant in one of our dialogues said: "Take courage."

- Agree to disagree. The guideline to embrace disagreements asks people to unpack their beliefs and opinions and try to identify what they're based on. The hope is that we'll better understand each other, not that we'll change another person's mind about an issue. That means that we may not be able to achieve consensus or clarity. Rather, we have to agree to disagree and be able to live with the lack of closure we might feel. The world we live in is complex, and the problems we face resist simple answers. Recognizing that complexity requires the ability to live with tensions, with paradoxes. My experience is not the same as yours, but mine is just as true as yours. Believing that something can be true and not true at the same time is not part of our way of thinking in the US. We tend to seek clear answers to problems, to try to explain away ambiguity and uncertainty, and to have the "best" solution. Talking about race—and ultimately doing something to improve racial understanding and eliminate racial disparities—requires us to learn to accept paradox and disagreement while we move forward in the conversation.

Writing this book has been both a labor of love and a struggle to absorb and live with what we have learned about Black history and experience and white people's complicity in that history and experience. We expect that it has been equally difficult at times for you to read this book. Several years ago, we did a presentation on interracial adoption for white people considering adopting a child of color or who had recently adopted a child of color. Our talk focused on the things we believe white people need to know about preparing children of color to live and thrive in our country. At the end of the workshop, a man raised his hand and said, "You've painted such a bleak picture of raising Black sons. Were there any joyful moments?" We were stunned. The experience of raising our children was constantly joyful. But it was also fraught with worries about racism. The same is true for talking about race. Amidst the guilt about white privilege, the fear of saying something wrong, the recognition of how complex and difficult the issues are, it's easy to forget that coming together with others to talk about race—really talk about it—can be cathartic, healing, and, ultimately, joyful.

To download The Reading Guide to *Let's Talk Race* visit
newsociety.com/pages/lets-talk-race-reading-guide

Endnotes

Introduction

1 Lori Tharps, "The Case for Black with a Capital B," *New York Times*, November 15, 2014.

2 Anne Price, "Spell It with a Capital 'B,'" Insight Center, October 1, 2019.

Chapter 1: Bridging the Chasm

1 Patti Hartigan, "Claudia Rankine Wants Us to Talk—Really Talk—about Race," *Boston Globe*, February 23, 2018.

2 See Marlene G. Fine and Fern L. Johnson, *The Interracial Adoption Option: Creating a Family Across Race* (Philadelphia: Jessica Kingsley, 2013).

3 Tanvi Misra, "A Complex Portrait of Rural America," CityLab, December 8, 2016.

4 Erica Gabrielle Foldy and Tamara R. Buckley, *The Color Bind: Talking (and Not Talking) about Race at Work* (New York: Russell Sage Foundation, 2014), 14.

5 Carol D. Leonnig and Jenna Johnson, "Anger Flows at Acquittal of George Zimmerman in Death of Trayvon Martin," *Washington Post*, July 14, 2013.

6 Bruce Drake, "Stark Racial Divisions in Reactions to Ferguson Police Shooting," Pew Research Center, August 18, 2014.

7 Philippe Lemoine, "Police Violence Against Black Men Is Rare," *National Review*, September 18, 2017.

8 Ronald S. Sullivan, Jr., "Black Lives Matter Occupies an Important Space," *Boston Globe*, September 1, 2015.

9 James B. Comey, "Hard Truths: Law Enforcement and Race," Speech at Georgetown University, February 12, 2015.

10 Evan Allen, "A Candid Look at Boston's Racial Divide," *Boston Globe,* November 19, 2016.

11 Ravi Somaiya, "Starbucks Ends Conversation Starters on Race," *New York Times*, March 22, 2015.

12 Errin Haines Whack, "Black Men Arrested at Starbucks Settle with the Company," Associated Press, May 2, 2018.

13 "Race in America 2019," Pew Research Center, April 9, 2019.

14 Link to data found in Nolan D. McCaskill, "'A Seismic Quake': Floyd Killing Transforms Views on Race," *Politico*, June 19, 2020.

15 United States Census Bureau, "Quick Facts 2019."

16 Eric Schmidt, "For the First Time, 90 Percent Completed High School or More," United States Census Bureau, July 31, 2018.

Chapter 2: Identifying Racism

1 Carl Zimmer, "A Single Migration from Africa Populated the World, Studies Find," *New York Times*, September 21, 2016.

2 Max Planck Institute for the Science of Human History, "Humans Did Not Stem from a Single Ancestral Population in One Region of Africa," *Science Daily*, July 11, 2018.

3 American Anthropological Association, "American Anthropological Association Statement on Race," May 17, 1998.

4 Jacqueline Jones, *A Dreadful Deceit* (New York: Basic Books, 2013), xii.

5 Thomas Chatterton Williams, *Self-Portrait in Black and White* (New York: W.W. Norton, 2019).

6 Derald Wing Sue, "Racial Microaggressions in Everyday Life," *Psychology Today*, October 5, 2010.

7 Ijeoma Oluo, *So You Want to Talk about Race* (New York: Seal Press, 2018), 164.

8 Ibram X. Kendi, *How to Be an Antiracist* (New York: One World, 2019), 47.

9 Trymaine Lee, "A Vast Wealth Gap, Driven by Segregation, Redlining, Evictions, and Exclusion, Separate White and Black America," *New York Times Magazine*, August 18, 2019.

10 Elise Gould, "State of Working America Wages 2018," Economic Policy Institute, February 20, 2019.

11 Linda Villarosa, "Who Lives? Who Dies? How Covid-19 Has Revealed the Deadly Realities of a Racially Polarized America," *New York Times Magazine*, May 3, 2020.

12 Ibid.

13 Lee, "A Vast Wealth Gap."

14 Associated Press, "Census Report: Broad Racial Disparities Persist," NBCNews.com, November 14, 2006.

15 William Darity Jr., Darrick Hamilton, Mark Paul, Alan Aja, Anne Price, Antonio Moore, and Caterina Chiopris, "What We Get Wrong about Closing the Racial Wealth Gap," Samuel Dubois Cook Center on Social Equity and Insight Center for Community Economic Development, April 2018, 3.

16 Laura Santhanam, "After Ferguson, Black Men Still Face the Highest Risk of Being Killed," *PBS Newshour,* August 9, 2019.

17 Taking Action Against Racism Media Group, "Internalized Racism," Society of Counseling Psychology, American Psychological Association Division 17, October 17, 2016.

18 Kenneth B. Clark and Mamie P. Clark, "Racial Identification and Preference among Negro Children," in *Readings in Social Psychology,* ed. E. L. Hartley (New York: Holt, Rinehart, and Winston, 1947).

19 Gitika Ahuja, "What a Doll Tells Us about Race," ABC News, March 31, 2009.

20 In Maggie Potapchuk, Sally Leiderman, Donna Bivens, and Barbara Major, "Flipping the Script: White Privilege and Community Building," MP Associates Inc. and the Center for Assessment and Policy Development, 2005, 50.

21 Stella Ting-Toomey, "Toward a Theory of Conflict and Culture," in *Communication, Culture, and Organizational Processes,* eds. William B. Gudykunst, Lea P. Stewart, and Stella Ting-Toomey (Beverly Hills, CA: Sage, 1985), 75.

22 Eva Hoffman, *Lost in Translation: A Life in a New Language* (New York: Penguin, 1989), 78.

23 Fern L. Johnson, *Speaking Culturally: Language Diversity in the United States* (Thousand Oaks, CA: Sage, 2000), 63–67.

24 Marsha Houston, "When Black Women Talk with White Women: Why Dialogues Are Difficult," in *Our Voices: Essays in Culture, Ethnicity, and Communication,* 4th ed., eds. Alberto Gonzalez, Marsha Houston, and Victoria Chen (Los Angeles: Roxbury, 2004).

25 Peggy McIntosh, "White Privilege: Unpacking the Invisible Knapsack," *Peace and Freedom,* July/August 1989.

26 Ta-Nehisi Coates, "My President Was Black," *The Atlantic,* Jan/Feb 2017, 57.

27 Oluo, *So You Want to Talk about Race,* 34.

Chapter 3: Erasing Our Race

1   Christopher Ingraham, "Three Quarters of Whites Don't Have Any Non-white Friends," *Washington Post,* August 25, 2014.

2   Celeste Ng, *Little Fires Everywhere* (New York: Penguin, 2017), 261.

3   Myles Spencer-Watson and Charisse Spencer, interview, *Story Corps,* National Public Radio, April 27, 2018.

4   See Timeline on the Fair Housing Center of Greater Boston website, "Historical Shift from Explicit to Implicit Policies Affecting Housing Segregation in Eastern Massachusetts."

5   Amy Traub, Laura Sullivan, Tatjana Meschede, and Thomas Shapiro, "The Asset Value of Whiteness: Understanding the Racial Wealth Gap," *Demos,* February 6, 2017.

6   Allie Jones, "Professors Are Less Likely to Mentor Female and Minority Students Especially in Business School," *The Atlantic,* April 22, 2014.

7   Joanne Taylor and Tatjana Meschede, "Inherited Prospects: The Importance of Financial Transfers for White and Black College-Educated Households Wealth Trajectories," *American Journal of Economic Sociology,* October 29, 2018.

8   Akilah Johnson, "That Was No Typo: The Median Net Worth of Black Bostonians Really Is $8," *Boston Globe,* December 11, 2017.

9   Rebecca Carroll, "What I See: Gloria Steinem, Shoulder to Shoulder with Women of Color," *New York Times,* December 10, 2018.

10 Joanna Walters, "Ron DeSantis Tells Florida Voters Not to 'Monkey This Up' by Choosing Gillum," *The Guardian,* August 29, 2018.

11 CNN-Time Magazine Poll, "Races Disagree on Impact of Simpson Trial," CNN, October 6, 1995.

12 Jeff Jacoby, "At Smith College, the Racist Incident That Wasn't," *Boston Globe,* August 6, 2018.

13 Callie Crossley, "The Smith College Incident Is What Everyday Racism Looks Like," WGBH News Commentary, August 12, 2018.

14 Paul Kivel, *Uprooting Racism: How White People Can Work for Racial Justice,* 2nd ed. (Gabriola Island, Canada: New Society Publishers, 2017), 35.

15 Maureen Milliken, "In Parting Words, Evans Utters Troubling Misreading of Black Lives Matter," letter to the editor, *Boston Globe,* August 7, 2018.

Chapter 4: Raising Your Racial IQ

1 Whether these Africans were enslaved or indentured servants is a matter of controversy. Clear, however, is that in Virginia, Africans were considered chattel by the late 1600s. See Nell Irvin Painter, "How We Think about the Term 'Enslaved' Matters," *The Guardian*, August 14, 2019.

2 Stacy Conradt, "12 Things You Might Not Know about Juneteenth," *Mental Floss*, June 19, 2019.

3 Melvin I. Urofsky, "Jim Crow Law," *Encyclopedia Britannica*.

4 Brian Duignan, "Plessy v. Ferguson," *Encyclopedia Britannica*.

5 Noreen Nasir, "In a Small Arkansas Town, Echoes of a Century-old Massacre," AP News, July 25, 2019.

6 Jesse J. Holland, "Hundreds of Black Deaths in 1919 Are Being Remembered," AP News, July 23, 2019.

7 Quoted in Jesse J. Holland.

8 Quoted in Dodie Kazanjian, "Amy Sherald," *Vogue*, August 2019.

9 Editorial Board, "Racial Isolation in Public Schools," *New York Times*, January 9, 2015.

10 James Vaznis, "Boston's Schools Are Becoming Resegregated," *Boston Globe*, August 4, 2018.

11 "7 of The Most Segregated School Systems in America," *Atlanta Black Star*, May 27, 2014.

12 Niraj Chokshi, "The Most Segregated Schools May Not Be in the States You'd Expect," *Washington Post*, May 15, 2014.

13 Southern Poverty Law Center, *Teaching Hard History: American Slavery*, February 2018.

14 Pew Research Center, "What Caused the Civil War?" May 18, 2011.

15 *Teaching Hard History*, 11.

16 American Council of Trustees and Alumni, "No U.S. History," July 2016.

17 Emily Deruy, "The Complicated Process of Adding Diversity to the College Syllabus," *The Atlantic*, July 20, 2016.

18 Annie E. Casey Foundation, "Race for Results Policy Report 2017: Kids Count," October 24, 2017.

19 Soheyla Taie, Rebecca Goldring, and Maura Spiegelman, "Characteristics of Public Elementary and Secondary School Teachers in the United States: Results from the 2015-16 National Teacher and Principal Survey," National Center for Education Statistics, June 2018, https://nces.ed.gov/pubs2017/2017072rev.pdf.

20 Desiree Carver-Thomas, "Diversifying the Teaching Profession: How to Recruit and Retain Teachers of Color," Learning Policy Institute, April 19, 2018.

21 Seth Gershenson, Stephen B. Holt, and Nicholas Papageorge, "Who Believes in Me? The Effect of Student Teacher Demographic Match on Teacher Expectations," W.E. Upjohn Institute for Employment Research, July 1, 2015.

22 Julie Landsman, *A White Teacher Talks about Race* (Lanham, MD: Roman and Littlefield, 2009), 28.

23 U.S. Department of Education Office for Civil Rights, "Data Snapshot: School Discipline," March 2014.

24 Elizabeth Arias and Jiaquan Xu, "United States Life Tables, 2017," *National Vital Statistics Reports* 68, no. 7 (June 24, 2019).

25 Ibid.

26 American Heart Association, "African Americans Live Shorter Lives Due to Heart Disease and Stroke," October 23, 2017.

27 Centers for Disease Control and Prevention, "Infant Mortality," March 27, 2019.

28 National Center for Biotechnology Information, *Chartbook with Special Feature on Racial and Ethnic Health Disparities*, May 2016.

29 Craig M. Hales, Margaret D. Carroll, Cheryl D. Fryar, and Cynthia L. Ogden, "Prevalence of Obesity among Adults and Youth: United States, 2015–2016." National Center for Health Statistics Data Brief, no. 288, October 2017.

30 Centers for Disease Control and Prevention, "U.S. Burden of Alzheimer's Disease, Related Dementias to Double by 2060," September 20, 2018.

31 Kenneth D. Kochanek, Elizabeth Arias, and Robert N. Anderson, "How Did Cause of Death Contribute to Racial Differences in Life Expectancy in the United States in 2010?" National Center for Health Statistics Data Brief, no. 125, July 2013.

32 American Heart Association, "African Americans Live Shorter Lives Due to Heart Disease and Stroke," October 23, 2017.

33 Garnette Cadogan, "Walking While Black," *Literary Hub*, July 8, 2016.

34 US Department of Justice, Federal Bureau of Investigation, "Crime in the United States, 2017," Fall 2018.

35 Samantha Artiga, Kendal Orgera, and Anthony Damico, "Changes in Health Coverage by Race and Ethnicity Since the ACA, 2010–2018," Henry J. Kaiser Family Foundation Issue Brief, March 5, 2020.

36 Association of American Medical Colleges, "Total U.S. Medical School Graduates by Race/Ethnicity," October 28, 2019.

37 Shamard Charles, "The Dearth of Black Men in Medicine Is Worrisome," NBC News article, May 5, 2019.

38 Cato Laurencin and Marsha Murray, "An American Crisis: The Lack of Black Men in Medicine," *Journal of Racial and Ethnic Health Disparities* 4, no. 3, (2017): 317–321.

39 Kelly M. Hoffman, Sophie Trawalter, Jordan R. Axt, and M. Norman Oliver, "Racial Bias in Pain Assessment and Treatment Recommendations, and False Beliefs about Biological Differences between Blacks and Whites," *Proceedings of the National Academy of Sciences*, April 4, 2016.

40 "Trump Bristles at Question about Police Killing Blacks," *Boston Globe*, July 15, 2020.

41 Erik Ortiz, "Inside 100 Million Police Traffic Stops," NBC News, March 13, 2019.

42 Sentencing Project, "Criminal Justice Facts," 2019.

43 Ibid.

44 Death Penalty Information Center, July 1, 2019, https://deathpenalty info.org/death-row/overview/demographics.

45 Sentencing Project, "Criminal Justice Facts."

46 Federal Bureau of Prisons, "Inmate Race," April 18, 2020.

47 Sentencing Project, "Criminal Justice Facts."

48 Nathaniel Lewis, *Mass Incarceration,* Peoples Policy Project, 2018.

49 John Grisham, "Eight Reasons for America's Shameful Number of Wrongful Convictions," *Los Angeles Times*, March 11, 2018.

50 Samuel R. Gross, Maurice Possley, and Klara Stephens, "Race and Wrongful Convictions in the United States," National Registry of Exonerations, March 7, 2017.

51 Tracy Jan, "Redlining Was Banned 50 Years Ago: It's Still Hurting Minorities Today," *Washington Post*, March 28, 2018.

52 Angela Hanks, Danyelle Solomon, and Christian E. Weller, "Systematic Inequality: How America's Structural Racism Helped Create the Black-White Wealth Gap," Center for American Progress, February 21, 2018.

53 Ibid.

54 Thai Jones, "Slavery Reparations Seem Impossible: In Many Places, They're Already Happening," *Washington Post*, January 31, 2020.

55 William Darity Jr. and A. Kirsten Mullen, "How Reparations for American Descendants of Slavery Could Narrow the Racial Wealth Divide," *Think,* NBC News, June 20, 2019.

56 Rachel L. Swarns, "Is Georgetown's $400,000-a-Year Plan to Aid Slave Descendants Enough?" *New York Times*, October 30, 2019.

57 Jones, "Slavery Reparations Seem Impossible."

58 Ta-Nehisi Coates, "The Case for Reparations," *The Atlantic*, June 2014, 71.

59 Ibid., 68.

Chapter 5: Recognizing Differences

1 Dahleen Glanton, "The Culture Clash at Prince Harry and Meghan Markle's Wedding Signaled Trouble Ahead," *Chicago Tribune*, January 13, 2020.

2 See Lisa J. Green, *African American English* (New York: Cambridge University Press, 2002).

3 John McWhorter, *Talking Back, Talking Black: Truths about America's Lingua Franca* (New York: Bellevue Literary Press, 2017), 18.

4 Geneva Smitherman, *Black Talk: Words and Phrases from the Hood to the Amen Corner* (Boston: Houghton Mifflin, 1994), 240.

5 Geneva Smitherman, *Talkin and Testifyin: The Language of Black America* (Boston: Houghton Mifflin, 1977), 134.

6 Sean Philip Cotter, "Gaffe-tastic Charlie Baker Does It Again, Calls Ayanna Presley Speech 'That Rant'," *Boston Herald*, January 20, 2020.

7 John McWhorter, "The 'ax' Versus 'ask' Question," *Los Angeles Times*, January 19, 2014.

8 Laura Alvarez Lopez, "Who Named Slaves and Their Children?" *Journal of African Culture* 27, no. 2 (2015).

9 Trevon Logan, "A Brief History of Black Names, from Perlie to Latasha," *The Conversation*, January 23, 2020.

10 David Zax, "What's Up with Black Names Anyway?" *Salon*, August 25, 2008.

11 Clarence Major, *Dictionary of Afro-American Slang* (NewYork: International Publishers, 1970), 84.

12 See Derrick Z. Jackson, "The N-word and Richard Pryor," *New York Times,* December 15, 2005.

13 Smitherman, *Black Talk*, 168.

14 Randall Kennedy, *Nigger: The Strange Career of a Troublesome Word* (New York: Pantheon, 2002).

15 See a detailed discussion of the case in Colleen Flaherty, "Too Taboo for Class?" *Inside Higher Ed*, February 1, 2019.

16 Chelsey Cox, "Another University of Oklahoma Professor Uses the 'N-word' During a Lecture," *USA Today*, February 27, 2020.

17 Marc Bain, "Ta-Nehisi Coates Gently Explains Why White People Can't Rap the N-word," *Quartz*, November 13, 2017.

18 Kimberly Sambol-Tosco, "Slavery and the Making of America: Historical Overview—Religion," WNET, 2004.

19 Ibid.

20 "In U.S., Decline in Christianity Continues at Rapid Pace," Pew Research Center, Religion and Public Life, October 17, 2019.

21 Julie E. Miller-Cribbs, "African-American Family Reunions: Directions for Future Research and Practice," *African American Research Perspectives* 10, no. 4 (2004), 160–173.

22 Kiana Keys, "Why Black Family Reunions Are a Special Tradition," *Sassy Plum*, April 17, 2017.

23 Samuel G. Freedman, "A Generational Divide Worn on Their Heads," *New York Times*, April 18, 2014.

24 Quoted in Christine Clarridge, "Sunday Hats: Special Beyond Easter," *Seattle Times,* April 13, 2017.

25 Quoted in Tricia Rose, *Black Noise* (Hanover, NH: University Press of New England, 1994) 38.

26 "The Dashiki: A Symbol of Africa," *Adunagow Magazine,* March 6, 2012.

27 "Afro-textured Hair," *Wikipedia,* https://en.wikipedia.org/wiki/Afro-textured_hair, accessed February 11, 2020.

28 Marita Golden, "My Black Hair: A Tangled Story of Race and Politics in America," *Quartz,* June 24, 2015.

29 Siraad Dirshe, "Respect Our Roots: A Brief History of Our Braids," *Essence,* June 27, 2018.

30 Jessica Cruel, "Wearing a Wig Doesn't Mean I Don't Love My Natural Hair," *Self,* January 29, 2018.

31 Crystal Aguh, "Hair Loss in Black Women: Tips from an Expert," Johns Hopkins Medicine, Health.

32 Joe Jurado, "A Texas Student Told to Cut His Dreadlocks If He Wants to Walk at Graduation," *The Root,* January 22, 2020.

33 *CBS This Morning,* January 24, 2020, https://www.cbsnews.com/news/dreadlocks-barbers-hill-texas-high-school-graduation-deandre-arnold-cut/.

34 Martenzie Johnson, "The Policing of Black Hair in Sports," *The Undefeated,* December 23, 2018.

35 Areva Martin, "The Hatred of Black Hair Goes beyond Ignorance," *Time,* August 23, 2017.

36 Mariel Padilla, "New Jersey Is Third State to Ban Discrimination Based on Hair," *New York Times,* December 20, 2019.

37 Sandra Garcia, "The Durag, Explained," *New York Times,* May 14, 2018.

Chapter 6: Better Talk

1 Leah Fessler, "Gloria Steinem Says These Are the Best Guidelines for Difficult Conversations," *Quartz at Work,* November 18, 2018.

2 Reni Eddo-Lodge, *Why I'm No Longer Talking to White People About Race* (New York: Bloomsbury Publishing, 2017), xiii.

3 Jeremy Stahl, "It's Like a Safari, and We're the Zebras," *Slate,* September 21, 2010.

4 Amber Ferguson, "'Come Meet a Black Person,' Says the Invitation to a Georgia Networking Event," *Washington Post,* November 15, 2017.

5 Poppy Noor, "Why Liberal White Women Pay a Lot of Money to Learn over Dinner How They're Racist," *The Guardian,* February 3, 2020.

6 Jonathan M. Metzl, *Dying of Whiteness: How the Politics of Racial Resentment Is Killing America's Heartland* (New York: Basic Books, 2018).

7 Francesco Duina, *Broke and Patriotic: Why Poor Americans Love Their Country* (Palo Alto, CA: Stanford University Press, 2017).

8 Robert Wuthnow, *The Left Behind: Decline and Rage in Rural America* (Princeton, NJ: Princeton University Press, 2018).

9 Court Stroud, "Everything You Need to Know About Urban Radio," *Forbes,* May 23, 2018.

10 Margaret Wilkerson Sexton, *The Revisioners: A Novel* (Berkeley, CA: Counterpoint Press, 2019), 244.

11 Renee Graham, "It's Not Up to Black People to Cure White Racism," *Boston Globe,* January 14, 2020.

12 Junot Diaz, "James McBride's 'Deacon King Kong' Is a Supercharged Urban Farce Lit Up by Thunderbolts and Rage," *New York Times Magazine,* February 29, 2020.

Index

About the Authors

F ERN L. JOHNSON, PhD, is Senior Research Scholar and Professor Emerita at Clark University, specializing in race, culture, and language. Her publications include *Speaking Culturally* and *Imaging in Advertising*, and many journal articles. She is a seasoned speaker and workshop facilitator. Fern co-authored, with Marlene Fine, *The Interracial Adoption Option*, which draws on their experience as white parents of African American sons. She lives near Boston, Massachusetts.

MARLENE G. FINE, PhD, is Professor Emerita at Simmons University, specializing in cultural diversity, leadership, and dialogue. She authored *Building Successful Multicultural Organizations*, and her articles appear in a broad range of journals. She is a seasoned speaker and workshop facilitator. Marlene co-authored, with Fern Johnson, *The Interracial Adoption Option*, which draws on their experience as white parents of African American sons. She lives near Boston, Massachusetts.

To download The Reading Guide to *Let's Talk Race* visit
newsociety.com/pages/lets-talk-race-reading-guide

A Note about the Publisher

New Society Publishers is an activist, solutions-oriented publisher focused on publishing books for a world of change. Our books offer tips, tools, and insights from leading experts in sustainable building, homesteading, climate change, environment, conscientious commerce, renewable energy, and more — positive solutions for troubled times.

We're proud to hold to the highest environmental and social standards of any publisher in North America. When you buy New Society books, you are part of the solution!

- We print all our books in North America, never overseas
- All our books are printed on **100% post-consumer recycled paper,** processed chlorine free, with low-VOC vegetable-based inks (since 2002)
- Our corporate structure is an innovative employee shareholder agreement, so we're one-third employee-owned (since 2015)
- We're carbon-neutral (since 2006)
- We're certified as a B Corporation (since 2016)

At New Society Publishers, we care deeply about *what* we publish — but also about *how* we do business.

ENVIRONMENTAL BENEFITS STATEMENT

New Society Publishers saved the following resources by printing the pages of this book on chlorine free paper made with 100% post-consumer waste.

TREES	WATER	ENERGY	SOLID WASTE	GREENHOUSE GASES
35	2,800	14	120	15,000
FULLY GROWN	GALLONS	MILLION BTUs	POUNDS	POUNDS

Environmental impact estimates were made using the Environmental Paper Network Paper Calculator 4.0. For more information visit www.papercalculator.org.

 Certified B Corporation

 FSC MIX Paper from responsible sources FSC® C016245

 new society PUBLISHERS www.newsociety.com